CAMERON DIAZ

CAMERON DIAZ

DANIEL O'BRIEN

Reynolds & Hearn Ltd
London

First published in 2002 by
Reynolds & Hearn Ltd
61a Priory Road
Kew Gardens
Richmond
Surrey TW9 3DH

A CIP catalogue record for this book is available from the British Library.

ISBN 1 903111 37 4

Designed by Paul Chamberlain.

Printed and bound in Malta by Interprint Ltd.

acknowledgements

My thanks to Pauline Dunham, Gary Kramer, Brian Neale, David O'Leary, Alison Powell, David Pratt, Richard Reynolds, Beth Richards, Adrian Rigelsford and Heather Shaw.

Front cover image © Rex Features.

Inside images © Rex Features and London Features International.

contents

introduction

There can't be many Hollywood actors who get their first break dancing with a green-faced loon. Even fewer have achieved stardom in a role that involves mistaking sperm for hair gel. From the start, Cameron Diaz has enjoyed an unusual movie career, to say the least. A premier member of the much derided model-turned-actress brigade, she has defied initial scepticism to become a major industry player.

Standing tall at 5'9", Diaz has undeniably striking features: sparkling blue eyes, naturally blonde hair, sensuous lips and cheekbones to die for. Yet good looks and print-ad celebrity are no guarantee of Hollywood success. When supermodel Cindy Crawford tried her luck with a starring role in *Fair Game* (1995), she made one of the least impressive film debuts of all time. Aside from her obvious sex appeal, Cameron Diaz has screen presence, energy, intelligence and a keen sense of humour. Unlike Crawford, she can also act, patiently learning her craft in low-key roles that weren't tailored to the multiplex crowd.

Cameron Diaz's rise to stardom took a mere four years, kicking off with her 1994 debut in *The Mask*. This live-action cartoon proved an ideal vehicle for star comedian Jim Carrey, whose manic, rubber-faced performance seemed at one with the special effects. Aged just 21, Diaz held her own as a sultry nightclub singer, attracting favourable attention. In 1995, *Empire* magazine placed Diaz at number 13 in its list of the 100 Sexiest Stars in Film History. Famously superstitious, Diaz may not have been too happy about the unlucky number. However, this was still a remarkable achievement for someone who'd been working in movies for barely a year.

In 1997, she co-starred in the hit comedy *My Best Friend's Wedding* and appeared on the cover of *Rolling Stone* magazine's 'Hot Issue'. A year later, Diaz made the big time with her starring role in the bad taste classic *There's Something About Mary*, one of 1998's biggest hits. The parade of gross-out jokes found an ideal balance in Diaz's good-natured, straight-faced performance. Even the stray semen couldn't faze her.

Early in her career, Cameron Diaz stated that she wanted to work with, and learn from, actors and directors she admired. To date, her co-stars include Jim Carrey, Keanu Reeves, Harvey Keitel, Julia Roberts, Ewan McGregor, Johnny Depp, Al Pacino, Tom Cruise and Leonardo DiCaprio. She's collaborated with such respected directors as Danny Boyle, Terry Gilliam, Oliver Stone, Spike Jonze, Cameron Crowe and Martin Scorsese. Not all the films have worked, yet Diaz always gives first-rate performances, often outshining more experienced co-stars.

The huge international success of *Charlie's Angels* (2000) and *Shrek* (2001) firmly established Cameron Diaz as one of Hollywood's biggest, most sought-after names. Her reputed $20 million pay cheque for *Charlie's Angels 2: Halo* (2003) matches the record for an actress, set by former co-star Julia Roberts on *Erin Brockovich* (2000). Very few male stars can command this kind of fee, which can only be supported by a run of solid-gold hits. Arnold Schwarzenegger's rumoured $30 million salary for *Terminator 3* (2002) says more about the franchise than the ageing action star. Diaz's achievement is remarkable, given that she has yet to carry a big-budget blockbuster movie single-handed.

Alongside the mega-hits, Cameron Diaz has pursued her commitment to more offbeat films, co-starring in *Being John Malkovich* (1999) and *Gangs of New York* (2002). She contributed a cameo to the wild and crazy *Fear and Loathing in Las Vegas* (1998) and even appeared in *Man Woman Film* (1999), a no-budget student movie made by an old friend. Diaz has worked with a number of first-time feature film directors, which in itself carries an element of risk. In the cases of *Being John Malkovich* and *Charlie's Angels*, it proved a highly successful gamble. On other occasions, Diaz was left to fend for herself.

Aside from a reputation for being late, Cameron Diaz has none of the usual movie star vices. True, she will only wash her face in Evian spring water, yet this level of skin care is hardly exclusive to the rich and famous. She also has a major fear of germs, and will open doors with her elbows rather than touch dirty, unsanitary handles. On the other hand, she eats well, especially Egg McMuffins with fries, drinks plenty and smokes her own hand-rolled cigarettes. Diaz is also renowned for her braying laugh, foul mouth and love of dirty jokes. She dislikes wearing a bra, as fans may have noticed, but denies that this is a provocative fashion statement: "It's really that I'm a tomboy at heart."

Cameron Diaz has been widely praised for her positive, enthusiastic working attitude. Her strong belief in this approach was confirmed during production on *My Best Friend's Wedding*, starring Julia Roberts:

One thing I realised from Julia – which I knew before, but was made very clear – is that

There's Something About Mary, once suggested that Diaz feared fame. She certainly dislikes the assumption that her private life is now public property. Interviewed by Bruce Kirkland in 1996, before *Mary* brought her Hollywood stardom, she hit out against press intrusion:

> **There is no reason why you should be comfortable with that just because you're a celebrity or an actor. I think that actors give enough of themselves on screen. That's their job. Their job is not to display what they do on their own time.**

This may now seem naïve, yet Diaz has appeared uncomfortable dealing with the media at times. Even studio-arranged press junkets were an ordeal for her. Diaz made her feelings clear to journalist Steve Tilley: "I get paid for publicity, and I act for free." Diaz also worried that, during the early days of *The Mask*, she'd been a little too open with the press:

> **My past is in print. Sometimes I wish it wasn't, but I'm living an incredible present, so it doesn't really have much of an effect on me if people keep digging it up.**

when you're the star of the film, the crew looks to you to set the tone of everyday work. So when you come into work, whatever it is that you're giving off, that is what the tone is going to be for the working conditions.

Though relaxed about the filmmaking process, Diaz doesn't underplay the amount of hard work involved. As she puts it: "Making movies is not easy. It's fun, but it becomes so complicated." One of these complications is the unrelenting media coverage of her personal life. Diaz has no problem with signing autographs, especially when she knows that fans have been waiting hours for a glimpse of her. As she explained to Canadian journalist Louis B Hobson: "It's sweet and flattering but it doesn't actually play into my life. I just consider it part of the job."

Diaz has less time for the tabloid press, a constant reminder of the downside of celebrity. Peter Farrelly, co-writer and co-director of

Away from the film set, Diaz's interests include motor racing, pool, bowling, heavy metal and *Monty Python's Flying Circus*. Her favourite writers are Raymond Carver and Charles Bukowski, hardly mainstream authors, and she loves Coen Brothers movies. Diaz has yet to work with the offbeat producer-director-writer team of Joel and Ethan

Above: Although her modelling days are behind her, Diaz appeared in this Japanese advertising campaign.

Above: *Although her modelling days are behind her, Diaz appeared in this Japanese advertising campaign.*

Coen. Hopefully, the day will come when the makers of *Fargo* (1995), *The Big Lebowski* (1998) and *O Brother, Where Art Thou?* (2000) create a decent role for her. Peter and Bobby Farrelly, the fraternal team behind *There's Something About Mary*, certainly hit the jackpot when they cast Diaz.

While by no means vain, Cameron Diaz is obviously comfortable with her looks, and fully aware of the attention they bring. She has little time for false modesty, as she explained to *Toronto Sun* reporter Bruce Kirkland:

I would sound like an idiot if I said I did not believe that people find me attractive. I made a living for many years doing so, looking beautiful, putting myself forward.

She is equally confident of her comedic gifts, telling journalist Liz Braun: "I've always made

people laugh. My mom is still the best audience. It's just so natural." On the other hand, Diaz rarely feels 100 per cent satisfied with her performances. Her standard response to seeing a finished movie is: "Now I know how I should have played that role. If only I'd known then what I know now."

Cameron Diaz denies having any kind of long-term career plan, other than picking the most interesting or fun roles available: "Ever since *The Mask*, I've considered myself lucky to be at the right place at the right time. It's all about serendipity." Interviewed by Louis B Hobson in October 1997, she still seemed awed by the whole Hollywood experience:

I learn something new about acting and about myself each time out. I never had any real aspirations to be an actress, but now that I've fallen into this career, I can't believe how lucky I am.

cartoon capers

Cameron Diaz was born in San Diego, California on 30 August 1972. Her Cuban-American father, Emilio Diaz, worked as an oil company foreman. Her mother, Billie, was an import/export broker. Billie Diaz had Anglo-German-Native American ancestry, which might explain Cameron's strong, highly distinctive features. There was one older sister, Chimene, now a parent in her own right. The Diaz family subsequently moved further up the West Coast to Long Beach, a major shipping port and home to the Queen Mary ocean liner. For the record, Cameron's Christian name is Gaelic for 'crooked stream'.

Diaz looks back on her childhood as extremely happy:

> My earliest memories are of laughter. I can shut my eyes and hear my father's laugh. My mother's is even more contagious. As a child, I did everything I could to make her laugh because it would make me laugh, too.

Nicknamed 'Cami', Diaz describes her younger self as "adventurous, independent and a tough kid", hitting baseballs in the street and getting into fights. Never one to back down, she wouldn't be intimidated by school bullies, making free with her fists more than once. She attributes this tough attitude to her father, along with her love of crude humour: "I get it from my dad. He's this macho foreman guy and I grew up wanting to be just like him." Tall for her age, and noticeably thin, Diaz earned the nickname 'Skeletor' after the skull-faced villain from the cartoon show *He-Man and the Masters of the Universe*. Imagination

Opposite: *Love at first sight. Who could resist green-faced charmer Jim Carrey in* The Mask?

obviously didn't run riot among her classmates. Perhaps for this reason, Diaz preferred to hang out with older kids.

She later attended Long Beach Polytechnic High School, whose former students included film star John Wayne and gangsta rapper Snoop Doggy Dogg. Diaz's own taste in music was strictly hard rock: Ozzy Osbourne, Metallica, Whitesnake, Ratt and AC/DC. Always keen on animals, Diaz had an early career ambition to be a zoologist. Her pets included two large snakes, fed on a supply of specially bred mice. Her first boyfriend, Lawrence May, drove a Skylark. Diaz once threatened to dump him if he let a Pacer overtake them. As anyone who's seen *My Best Friend's Wedding* or *Charlie's Angels* can testify, Cameron Diaz likes her driving fast and furious.

Emilio and Billie Diaz had a relaxed attitude to child-rearing, taking Chimene and Cameron to parties and rock concerts from an early age. When Cameron attended her first rock gig, a Van Halen concert, Billie came along. To this day, Diaz remains extremely close to her immediate family:

> My family is my anchor. I couldn't think of doing anything without my family. They've supported me in every choice I've made. I never want it to look as if I'm abusing their faith in me.

For the teenage Cameron Diaz, Long Beach had the advantage of being just an hour's train journey from Los Angeles. At the age of 16, she gatecrashed a fashionable Hollywood party, passing herself off as 21. Many of the male guests turned out to be "sleazy guys hitting on girls by pretending they were agents for model-

Tall, blonde, blue-eyed women were thin on the ground in Japan, and Cameron's looks at least had novelty value. Her parents did not oppose this potentially risky expedition, and their faith in Cameron proved well-founded most of the time. As Diaz later explained:

Believe me, you can get into a lot of trouble being 16 years old in a foreign country with no adult telling you when to come home.

Sharing a two-bedroom apartment, Diaz certainly enjoyed her new life in Japan, where "models are treated like rock stars". This initial taste of celebrity included some of its more questionable aspects. Interviewed at the time of *The Mask*'s release, Diaz admitted to 'experimenting' with illicit drugs during her time in the Far East.

Cameron Diaz soon found regular employment as a fashion model for magazines. She would spend a total of five years living and working abroad in various countries. On leaving Japan, Cameron picked up assignments in Australia, France, Mexico and Morocco. By Diaz's own admission, her new, liberated, globe-trotting lifestyle had its hairy moments. The worst of these was a bout of alcohol poisoning in Australia when she was 18. Shooting a Coke advert on Bondi Beach, Diaz relaxed after hours with a succession of exotic cocktails, followed by some vintage Japanese sake. Violently ill for the next 24 hours, she claims to have lost seven pounds.

In front of the camera, Cameron Diaz had few bad experiences, though she later regretted a series of nude photographs taken in

Left: Cameron Diaz pictured in 1988. Is this the face of a future Hollywood star?

ling firms." Dressed in a jump-suit and high heels, Diaz didn't think she looked a likely prospect for catwalk stardom. Nevertheless, she was approached by a man, Jeff Dunas, who claimed to be both a top photographer and an agent for the major-league Elite Modelling Agency. Taken with Cameron's looks, he offered to find her high-profile, highly paid work as a print model. A wary Diaz accepted Dunas' business card and, after consulting with her family, agreed to make an appointment with the agency. While the whole thing sounded like a dubious chat-up line, Dunas quickly proved his credentials. Within a week, Cameron Diaz had signed up with Elite. Her professional modelling debut, an advertisement for *Teen* magazine, paid $125.

Shortly afterwards, Cameron left the family home, and the United States. Determined to further her new career in modelling, she travelled to Japan, accompanied by another aspiring model one year her junior.

Above: *Tina Carlyle struts her stuff in The Mask.*

1991 during her stay in Japan. She'd already worked with the photographer, who assured Diaz that the pictures were strictly for her personal portfolio. As Diaz explained it: "I was very young and this photographer took advantage of my naïveté." Once she became a big name, it was inevitable that the pictures would see the light of day. A few years later, they were published in *Celebrity Sleuth* magazine, subsequently appearing on the same outfit's website. Out on the publicity trail for *A Life Less Ordinary* (1997), Diaz seemed cool about the matter: "It was my fault because I gave permission. I thought at the time I could handle the nudity thing because I'm not afraid of my body." Significantly, Diaz has never appeared naked on screen, insisting that a nude scene be dropped from *There's Something About Mary*.

In between the print modelling assignments, Diaz found time to finish high school, graduating in the Long Beach Polytechnic Class of 1990. The previous year, aged 17, she

acquired a serious boyfriend, video producer Carlos de La Torre, with whom Diaz later shared a Hollywood apartment.

In 1993, Diaz returned to California for good. Now 21, she continued to work as a model. After just a few years in the business, she'd appeared on the covers of *Mademoiselle* and *Seventeen* and done adverts for Levi's, LA Gear, Coca Cola, Nivea and Calvin Klein. Having started off at $125, her standard fee reached $2000 a day. In 1994, the year of her feature film debut, Diaz appeared in a television advert for Salon Selectives. She could also be seen in MTV's 'Behind the Video' programme on REM's 'The Great Beyond'. She had succeeded way beyond her initial dreams.

I loved modelling because it allowed me to travel, meets lots of interesting people and make good money for someone so young. Still, I knew something was missing...

Cameron Diaz's search for a career beyond magazine and catalogue adverts ended with *The Mask* (1994). For this enjoyable New Line comedy, she played a *femme fatale* with a heart of gold and some hot dance moves. It's not the most original or challenging of roles, yet Diaz shines on the screen. Even Jim Carrey has to stop and take notice. Diaz had to work hard to win the part, a fully fledged co-starring role. Aware that modelling was not a long-term prospect, she decided to audition for the film after seeing the script on her TV ad agent's desk. According to one version of events, the agent initially suggested that she try out for a smaller part, which seemed a more realistic proposition for a film novice.

Lacking any previous acting experience, professional or otherwise, Diaz did not rate her chances very highly. On the other hand, New Line were testing several models for the film, more concerned with looks and screen presence than acting ability. Her initial audition impressed the producers, yet proved inconclusive. While the casting agents and director Charles Russell liked Diaz, her newcomer status made her a risk. Unable to make up their minds, New Line called her back to re-audition 11 times. Diaz did line readings with star Jim Carrey and tried out the dance numbers required for her character, a nightclub artiste. After a while, Diaz felt that the film's choreographer was using her as his unofficial, unpaid rehearsal partner for the dance sequences. This brought out her stubborn streak. Eager as she was to work on the film, Diaz did not want to be exploited:

Anything the filmmakers wanted, I would do. But it got to the point where I

Opposite: *Teasing the camera in* The Mask.

said, 'You know what? I'm not doing it anymore. I'm not gonna go practice with the choreographer so that he knows the steps he's gonna teach the real girl who gets the job'.

Sensitive to Diaz's concerns, Charles Russell eventually persuaded *The Mask*'s producers to go with the hard-working newcomer, who'd more than proved her ability. Even after the intensive dramatic and dancing work-outs, Diaz was genuinely surprised to be given the role, quickly signing up for acting classes.

The Mask is essentially a contemporary reworking of *Dr Jekyll and Mr Hyde*, with the emphasis on rapid-fire slapstick comedy. Independent outfit New Line developed the $18 million production as a showcase for comedian Jim Carrey, who'd recently scored a surprise hit with *Ace Ventura: Pet Detective* (1994). Based on characters from the Dark Horse comics, the story takes place in Edge City. Carrey plays downtrodden bank clerk Stanley Ipkiss. Diaz is Tina Carlyle, a nightclub singer and gangster's moll just dying to be reformed by love.

During production, Cameron Diaz noticed that Jim Carrey seemed very comfortable with his star status: "Jim loved it when hundreds of young fans lined up to see him come to the set… He thinks that's cool for himself and for them." In contrast, Diaz had been working on the film for over a month before the importance of the project hit her:

I didn't realise it was a fairly large film that I was a part of. Halfway through I was going, 'Is there any place that my mom and dad can see this film?' and they're going, 'Cameron, at the theatres.' I had no idea. Durrrrrr. I'm blonde. I'm allowed.

While Diaz later treated this 'shock' discovery as a joke, at the time she became worried that she'd screw up and let the filmmakers down. This sense of pressure led to her developing an ulcer. Having discovered the hard way that she was up to the job, Diaz made it through to the end of filming. Twenty film appearances later, Cameron Diaz still suffers from stress-related stomach pains before starting work on a new movie. Thankfully, she can now calm herself down with special breathing techniques.

It's fair to say that *The Mask* owes a lot to its special effects, provided by George Lucas' Industrial Light and Magic company, with special make-up by Greg Cannom. The actual plot is pretty basic. Stanley Ipkiss is a lovable loser, used and abused by garage mechanics, bank colleagues, nightclub bouncers, ill-tempered landladies and ambitious reporters. In need of an escape from reality, Ipkiss has a cartoon fixation, especially the work of Tex Avery. One of the greatest animation directors, Avery developed the characters of Daffy Duck and Bugs Bunny at Warner Bros during the late 1930s. Avery subsequently joined MGM, making some of the most inventive, energetic, outrageous, subversive and generally dazzling cartoon shorts of all time. *The Mask* pays particular homage to *Red Hot Riding Hood* (1943), with Diaz standing in for the original singing-dancing 'Red'. She does a pretty good job.

Ipkiss discovers an ancient mask which releases the wild, irrepressible part of his personality. This involves Stanley becoming the

in on Cameron Diaz, taking in her legs, cleavage and highly symbolic red dress. There is even a little slow-motion hair-tossing, a Diaz speciality that reached its zenith with *Charlie's Angels* (2000). Though looking more than good here, Diaz would subsequently shed a few pounds, hopefully by choice rather than Hollywood dictate.

One of Ipkiss' less inhibited co-workers sniffs Tina's discarded coat, which is a bit scary. Admiring Stanley's Rorsach-effect tie, Tina claims to see a naked lady on a horse in the abstract patterns. Could it be she's just trying to unsettle the already panting Stanley? Mopping down her neck, Tina adjusts her handbag, which contains a camera secretly filming the bank for a forthcoming raid.

Cameron's wardrobe for *The Mask* is top-of-the-range, including a dress with vertical black and white stripes, a white blouse and long black skirt, and a black evening dress adorned with red piping. (Tina's only questionable fashion choice is a black and white checked jacket worn with blue jeans. Make up your mind.) Decked out in a sparkling mini dress, Tina's sensational nightclub act proves that she's more than just a mobster's trophy. As a newspaper headline puts it: 'Bombshell Explodes at Coco Bongo'. It matters little that Diaz was doubled for some of the dance moves, or that her singing had to be dubbed. One major career change at a time.

Ipkiss dreams of a romantic encounter with Tina, who declines his proffered lips, licking his right ear instead. Even this unorthodox show of affection is just too good to be true, Stanley waking up to find his dog licking him in bed. Yick. Stanley later throws away his press cutting

cartoon character of his fantasies, capable of unlimited animated mayhem. As Stanley puts it: "Smokin'!" The mask seems to be connected to Loki, the Norse god of mischief. This subplot was clarified in a deleted prologue featuring 11th century Vikings, who dump the Mask in the sea during a brief visit to the American continent.

Tina Carlyle is first seen running into Ipkiss' bank from a downpour. As she bends over to adjust her footwear, the camera tracks

Above: *With boyfriend Carlos de La Torre at the premiere of* The Mask.

about Tina's sensational Coco Bongo debut, feeling that he has no chance of catching her eye.

As the Mask, things are different: "Hold on sugar! Daddy's got a sweet tooth tonight!" Watching Tina in action at the Coco Bongo, the Mask cannot restrain himself. His jaw drops down several feet, closely followed by his unrolling tongue. His eyes pop out on stalks and his heart beats its way out of his chest. Many Diaz fans feel the same way. Overwhelmed by both the Mask's dancing and his kiss, Tina starts to question her criminal associations. It helps that her brutish, if upwardly mobile, gangster lover, Dorian (Peter Greene), is a Badfella of the first order. He's the kind of villain who'll shoot up a cute giant-sized piggy bank filled with money for war orphans. Inevitably, Tina comes to appreciate Stanley without the Mask, even if his idea of a romantic evening is a date in Landfill Park. Unlike Dorian, and just about every other man she's met, Stanley treats Tina as a person, not a "party favour".

Punching one bad guy in the face, Tina is no passive damsel in distress. During the climactic showdown between Stanley and Dorian, the latter is wearing the Mask to begin with, resembling a less friendly version of *Shrek*. Tied to a fake palm tree with explosives placed around the base, Tina tricks her ex-boyfriend into removing the Mask with the promise of one last kiss. It's a good offer. With the Mask back on his face, Stanley just can't be beaten. The film freeze-frames on the Stanley-Tina clinch, the Mask hurled back into Edge City river.

New Line marketed *The Mask* with the tagline: 'From Zero To Hero.' Cameron Diaz received a special 'introducing' credit, the kiss of death for many a budding film career,

though largely because the debutantes involved are either hopelessly miscast or utterly useless. Released in the United States on 29 July 1994, *The Mask* proved a smash hit, grossing $120 million in the US and $321 million worldwide. The film's huge success confirmed Jim Carrey's new superstar status. Director Charles Russell went on the make the big-budget Arnold Schwarzenegger action movie *Eraser* (1996). Diaz picked up three 1995 MTV Movie Award nominations, for Best Breakthrough Performance, Best Dance Sequence (shared with Jim Carrey) and Most Desirable Female. Not a bad start.

While Cameron Diaz held her own against both Jim Carrey and the barrage of digital effects wizardry, *The Mask* did not bring her overnight stardom by any means. Some sections of the press dismissed Diaz as just another model-turned-actress, with little to distinguish her from the pack. For all her good looks and charisma, several reporters expressed doubt that Diaz would ever make another film. After a couple of minor setbacks, she would quickly prove them wrong. While *The Mask* doesn't appear to be one of Diaz's favourite films, she remains grateful for this early break into movies. Interviewed by Bruce Kirkland in 1996, Diaz acknowledged her debt to Charles Russell and Jim Carrey:

What *The Mask* did for me was give me the opportunity to meet people I wouldn't normally get to meet as a beginner: executives, directors, writers and producers. I was given a lot better material than I probably would have been given without the success of a film such as *The Mask*.

sex and death

Opposite: *Diaz indulged her passion for motor sports at the Toyota Pro-Celeb Race in April 1995.*

Rather than coasting on the back of *The Mask*, accepting the next *femme fatale* part that came along, Cameron Diaz opted to lower her Hollywood profile for a while. Lacking both film experience and technique, she turned to the independent, low-budget section of the industry, seeing it as a valuable training ground.

Things could have been very different, however, if injury and rejection hadn't intervened. New Line offered Diaz a co-starring role in *Mortal Kombat* (1995) as an immediate follow-up to *The Mask*. Around the same time, she auditioned for a major part in the offbeat crime thriller *Things to Do in Denver When You're Dead* (1995). Andy Garcia starred as Jimmy the Saint, a former criminal who reluctantly agrees to take on One Last Job. Needless to says, things go horribly wrong, leaving Jimmy and his hand-picked gang at the mercy of a contract killer. The supporting cast included Christopher Walken, as The Man with the Plan, and Steven Buscemi as Mr Shhh the hitman. Diaz tested for the role of Dagney, Jimmy's oddly named love interest. In the event, the part went to Gabrielle Anwar, who'd appeared opposite Al Pacino in *Scent of a Woman* (1992). Despite mostly favourable reviews, *Things to Do…* failed to become a *Pulp Fiction* or *Usual Suspects*-style cult hit.

Diaz had more luck with New Line's film version of *Mortal Kombat*, one of the most popular video game punch-ups. *Highlander* star Christopher Lambert took the lead role of Rayden, benevolent god of the Outworld, who must recruit human fighters for a brutal tournament that offers Planet Earth as the main prize. Impressed by Diaz's looks and athleticism, the producers cast her as Sonya Blade, one third of Rayden's all-new monster-fighting team. Shortly before the start of production, Diaz broke her wrist during a training session for the film, when she hit her karate instructor too hard on the head. No longer up to the demanding action sequences, she dropped out of the film. New Line recast the role with Bridgette Wilson, who at least matched Diaz in height.

Mortal Kombat turned out to be a pretty good action movie, imaginatively shot and designed, though both Wilson and Lambert had the sense to pass on the mediocre sequel *Mortal Kombat 2: Annihilation* (1997). Bridgette Wilson subsequently appeared in the lame offerings *I Know What You Did Last Summer* (1997), *House on Haunted Hill* (1999) and *The Wedding Planner* (2001), but remains best known for her relationship with tennis champion Pete Sampras. In retrospect, it's arguable that Diaz was fortunate to miss out on *Mortal Kombat*. Playing another comic book-style character so soon after *The Mask* could have typecast her in action roles that required little acting ability. Viewers anxious to see Diaz in kickass mode were later rewarded with *Charlie's Angels*.

It's been suggested that Diaz's health problems on both *The Mask* and *Mortal Kombat* made some producers wary of hiring her, and that, rather than *choosing* to develop her talent in low-key, non-mainstream films, she had little say in the matter. Still earning a good living from high-profile modelling assignments, Diaz agreed to play a more challenging role in *The Last Supper* (1995). Directed by Stacy Title, this black comedy

I did *The Last Supper* simply to get the opportunity to work with other actors. I'd never had any other experience [of] acting other than *The Mask*.

Her co-stars on the film included Jonathan Penner, Annabeth Gish, *Seinfeld* actor Jason Alexander, Charles Durning and Ron Perlman. Penner also served as the film's co-executive producer and second unit director. There's dedication for you. Diaz found making *The Last Supper* a pleasant, non-stressful experience. As she explained to Bruce Kirkland:

It was an ensemble piece... I didn't have to carry the load of an entire film and I got to learn from really incredibly talented actors who gave me a lot of help and support.

In *The Last Supper*, five house-sharing graduate students give their liberal views a lethally pro-active spin. Anyone with offensive opinions, whether moral or political, is a legitimate target for extermination. The first death is an accident, an unexpected dinner guest killed after he turns violent. Truck-driver Zack (Bill Paxton) confirms everyone's worst prejudices about Deep South Good Ol' Boys. A racist, anti-Semitic Holocaust denier, he pulls a knife, threatens rape, breaks an arm and ends up stabbed in the back. Once the housemates have got over their initial shock at this turn of events, they begin to appreciate its positive side. A succession of repellent, hate-filled bigots are invited to a hearty last meal, then ceremonially 'executed' by poisoning. The victims include a homophobic priest

tackles such heavy issues as political expediency and moral choice. The film is uneven in tone, throwing in elements of black comedy, satire, fantasy and morality tale. The end result is strangely likeable, given the subject matter. It certainly makes Iowa seem a more intriguing, if dangerous place.

Cameron Diaz didn't have any particular interest in *The Last Supper*'s themes or storyline. What she did appreciate was a good chance to hone her acting skills without the sense of pressure she'd felt during the *Mask* shoot:

Above: *Jude debates the finer points of justifiable homicide in* The Last Supper.

(Durning), who regards AIDS as God's vengeance on the 'degenerate' gay community, and a pro-life activist prepared to kill doctors who 'murder' unborn babies by carrying out abortions. After the killing of a librarian with a poor taste in classic literature, some of the group start to question their actions.

There's a lot to enjoy in *The Last Supper*, not least KC and the Sunshine Band singing 'I'm Your Boogie Man' over the opening titles. While Dan Rosen's script doesn't fully develop or sustain its weighty theme, the ideas raised are provocative. The title is an obvious reference to Christ's Last Supper prior to his arrest, trial and crucifixion. The names of the leading characters are taken from the New Testament too: Paulie/Paul (Gish), Marc/Mark (Penner), Luke (Courtney B Vance), Pete/Peter (Ron Eldard) and Jude/Judas (Diaz). Contrary to expectations, Jude doesn't betray her fellow executioners. These self-styled disciples of death use wine poisoned with arsenic, a twist on the Christian mass. The last suppers always take place on a Sunday, the traditional day of worship. On the other hand, the housemates make their big moral decisions during heavy drinking sessions, which is a whole different kind of spiritual experience.

There are a number of flaws. Some of the black humour seems misplaced. Zack belches as he dies, undercutting what should be a truly disturbing moment. He's later revealed to have been a child molester, rapist and murderer. This would seem to endorse the liberal vigilante's actions. However, none of their subsequent guests, all hand-picked for 'execution', have hurt anyone. On the other hand, the human fertiliser does wonders for the tomatoes growing in the back garden.

Though first-billed on the opening credits, Cameron Diaz is by no means the film's star, sharing centre stage with her fellow cast members. Her character, Jude, has been described as 'uber-cool', which is true up to a point. A psychology graduate, Jude makes (deliberately?) lame jokes about masturbation. Compared to *There's Something About Mary*, this is mild stuff. At one point, she is accused of being a "fashion victim", presumably a reference to Diaz's modelling career. *The Last Supper* poses a classic ethical dilemma: if it were possible to go back in time and meet the young Adolf Hitler before he moved into politics, would it be morally justifiable to kill him? The death of a then-innocent man could prevent the rise of Nazi Germany, the Second World War and the Final Solution, thereby saving millions of lives. Jude has a simple answer: "I would kill the bastard. Slowly."

At first, Jude seems just as laid-back about the non-hypothetical killings, even finishing a meal with one recently dead body still at the table. Clumsily wresting a kitchen knife from the back of a teetotal victim, Jude doesn't look so cool. She later plants wreaths around the graves, tears in her eyes. The morally correct executions are taking their toll. Jude draws the line at killing a naïve teenage girl hung up on family values and the evils of mandatory sex education. As the group's solidarity starts to crumble, it's Jude who forces the now-fanatical Luke to back down. Diaz's anguished performance suggests a greater depth to her character than the script does. Judging from the closing credits, a scene featuring Jude as a young girl was filmed but cut from the finished movie.

Left: *Don't touch the blue bottle! A self-satisfied Jude in* The Last Supper.

Throughout *The Last Supper*, there are regular cutaways to obnoxious television pundit Norman Arbuthnot (Ron Perlman), who stirs up his studio audience with misogynist, racist and homophobic remarks. Away from the cameras, Arbuthnot seems more thoughtful, moderate and reasonable than the five self-appointed Liberal Vigilantes. He even suggests that talking to the young Adolf Hitler might have better long-term consequences than simply killing him. The implied twist ending suggests that the execution committee have been given a taste of their own bad medicine. Pay careful attention to the last painting shown.

The Last Supper premiered at the Toronto Film Festival on 8 September 1995. The film didn't go on release in the United States until 5 April 1996 and grossed only $443,000 at the American box-office. British audiences had to wait until 23 August, a sure sign that distributors had little faith in the film's commercial appeal. On the plus side, they came up with a decent tagline: 'Eat… drink… and be buried…'

Having committed herself to acting,

Cameron Diaz also made some major changes in her personal life. In 1995 she ended her relationship with Carlos de La Torre, after five years of "semi-engagement". Shortly afterwards, Diaz began dating fellow actor George Clooney, then best known as the star of the hit medical soap opera *ER*. Clooney's big screen career was just starting to take off, with films like the cult guns'n'vampires epic *From Dusk Till Dawn* (1995). Neither Diaz nor Clooney were looking for serious commitment at the time, and the relationship ended amicably after three months.

While hardly a box-office sensation, *The Last Supper* proved that Cameron Diaz could act. It also confirmed her commitment to films rather than fleeting stardom. Diaz's third movie, *She's the One* (1996), suggested that she could rise above indifferent material. The script deals with the absurdly tangled love lives of the male-dominated Fitzpatrick family, blue collar Irish-American Catholics from Brooklyn, New York. This is a reasonable premise, yet the movie is neither as smart nor perceptive as it thinks it is. Unconcerned with establishing a wholesome screen image,

Diaz did get to play her first out-and-out queen bitch, turning in an accomplished performance despite the poor script.

Writer-director-star Edward Burns had covered more or less the same territory with his debut film, *The Brothers McMullen* (1995), which attracted favourable attention. Burns recruited fellow *McMullen* cast members Mike McGlone and Maxine Bahns for *She's the One*, alongside better-known faces such as Diaz, *Friends* star Jennifer Aniston and *Frasier* co-star John Mahoney. Veteran Hollywood star Robert Redford served as the film's co-executive producer, helping to secure the modest $3.5 million budget and a distribution deal with industry giant Twentieth Century Fox.

Burns plays Mickey Fitzpatrick, probably the only white, English-speaking taxi driver in New York. In the best – or possibly worst – fairy tale tradition, he picks up a fare, the beguiling Hope (Bahns), and embarks on an impulsive whirlwind romance, ending up married to a woman he barely knows. Mickey's younger brother Francis (McGlone) is an ambitious Wall Street executive and utter prick. A workaholic and control freak, he is obsessed with money, status, 'proper' conduct and social convention. Francis' non-stop work routine appears to be hurting his marriage to the delightful Renee (Aniston). In fact, their non-existent sex life is a result of his infidelity. Convinced that Francis has 'turned' gay, Renee is reduced to pleasuring herself with a vibrator. There is something mildly subversive about Aniston, so wholesome as *Friends*' Rachel, frankly discussing sex aids, though the script flogs the idea to exhaustion.

As the best known cast member, Jennifer Aniston received top billing in *She's the One*, Diaz having to make do with fourth place. Burns cast Diaz as Heather Davis, Mickey's ex-fiancée and Francis' current lover. Before she even appears, we know that Heather is bad news, a cold hearted heart-breaker. Despite Mickey's devotion, Heather proved unfaithful, sending him into a three-year crisis, drifting aimlessly around the country.

When Diaz first read the script for *She's the One*, she was immediately taken with Heather: "I loved her right off. I even loved her deviousness." At the same time, she felt the character lacked depth and sympathy: "I thought, if Mickey could love this person, there must be something about her worth caring about." Edward Burns credits Diaz with developing the character to a new level, yet Heather remains highly dislikeable in the finished film.

Going in for slicked-back hair and shirts with green and white stripes, cab driver Mickey is not the most dashing individual on the surface. Heather's inability to appreciate his fine inner qualities shows just how shallow she is, not to mention amoral, manipulative and selfish. Not content with screwing her ex-boyfriend's brother, Heather also has an older lover, who is much better in bed than Francis.

To her credit, Diaz's performance does persuade the viewer that Francis would dump the seemingly perfect Renee for Heather, if only because she shares his lack of feelings and values. Heather and Francis expect everyone to live down to their standards, resenting any show of decency or real emotion, even from each other. Their post-coital conversation is not exactly affectionate:

Left: *Heather Davis plays games with the Fitzpatrick brothers, ex-fiancé Mickey (Edward Burns, left) and current lover Francis (Mike McGlone, right) in* She's the One.

**HEATHER: I faked my orgasm with you.
FRANCIS: So?**

Writer-director Burns stacks the cards so much in Mickey's favour that Heather has no chance of winning audience sympathy. She even begrudges Mickey his old television set, which she could replace 100 times over on her Wall Street salary. Given that Mickey's scuzzy apartment lacks electricity, it's more of a moral victory than a practical one.

One of the film's major revelations is that Heather prostituted herself to pay her way through college, performing oral sex on wealthy clients. Burns could have used this plot point to humanise the character, making her a damaged, embittered victim of economic deprivation and male exploitation, shielding her vulnerability behind a mask of cool indifference. As it turns out, she barely seems bothered. Of course, Mickey, a decent, understanding kind of guy, has never had a problem with this interesting piece of Heather's past history. Discovering Heather's relationship with Francis, however, Mickey refers to her as a "whore". Unfortunately, there's nothing in the movie to make audiences disagree. Diaz felt that the character was "an extreme of what women think they should be, about women taking power". Maybe so, but if Heather is supposed to have hidden depths and sensitivity, it doesn't show.

Even Francis has more integrity than Heather, refusing to have sex with his wife now that he's fallen for another woman. This is a skewed kind of moral logic, but better than none at all. When Heather presents Francis with the same expensive wristwatch that she once gave to Mickey, it's clear that she's just plain bad. Despite this, Mickey finds himself still drawn to Heather, who casually offers a new start to their relationship, unconcerned with Mickey's recent marriage (or her two on-going liaisons). This time around, the yuppie *femme fatale* does not get her way. Heather ends up marrying her older lover, a loyal former customer from her part-time prostitution days. The implication is that they are perfectly suited to each other, as neither will have any foolish romantic illusions about the nature of their relationship. Regular sex in return for status, money and security, without all the usual hypocrisy, is better than nothing. Ain't love grand?

In fairness, *She's the One* is not a total washout, boasting a good Tom Petty soundtrack and a handful of decent one-liners. John Mahoney, who plays Mr Fitzpatrick senior, is amusing, offering his sons constant fatherly advice that invariably proves unhelpful. The family own a fishing boat called 'The Fighting Fitzpatricks', which turns out to be more than an idle boast, Mickey and Francis engaging in a brotherly grudge match over the Heather affair. Reluctant to fight, Mickey floors his arrogant, over-confident sibling with one punch. Mrs Fitzpatrick remains unseen, as does Heather's older man, the former eventually leaving her husband for an elderly hardware store owner. The happy ending prompts a big 'so what?' response, Mickey apparently reconciled with his father, brother and wife, their new understanding cemented by a bonding fishing trip.

Released in the United States on 23 August 1996, *She's the One* grossed $9.5 million during its North American theatrical release. At around $1 million per week, this doesn't sound very impressive, yet the film turned a small profit. A number of reviewers found the movie offensively chauvinistic in tone, verging on outright misogyny in the case of Diaz's character. *Empire* magazine saw nothing to get mad about, describing *She's the One* as "an easy-going diversion". *Toronto Sun* reporter Bruce Kirkland suggested that Diaz, rather than the better-known Jennifer Aniston, was the one to watch: among the "clutch of rising young Hollywood femme fatale stars [sic]", she looked like becoming a serious rival to big names Julia Roberts, Demi Moore and Sandra Bullock. A few years later, only Roberts was still in the running.

Cameron Diaz did a lot better with her next released film, the underrated *Feeling Minnesota* (1996). This was a co-production between *Mask* producers New Line and actor Danny De Vito's Jersey Films, which had a hand in *Pulp Fiction* (1994). De Vito served as an executive producer alongside Michael Shamberg and *Last Supper* director Stacy Sher. Diaz remained on good terms with Sher, who'd guided her through her first 'proper' acting role. The budding star even claimed that:

I never would have been able to do *Feeling Minnesota* if I had not done *The Last Supper*. I would have completely fallen apart and they would have kicked me off the set.

Feeling Minnesota was written and directed by former actor Steven Baigelman, making his behind-the-camera debut. The movie takes its offbeat title from a Soundgarden song lyric: 'I just looked in the mirror, things aren't looking so good. I'm looking California and feeling Minnesota.' Close to the Canadian border, Minnesota has a reputation for being cold and depressing. Soundgarden get an acknowledgment in the closing credits, not that many viewers would still be watching by the time it comes up.

Aside from Diaz, the film featured Keanu Reeves, Vincent D'Onofrio, pop singer Courtney Love and ageing funnyman Dan Aykroyd. Reeves was Diaz's first big-name co-star since Jim Carrey, two years earlier. Several flops on from the hit *Speed* (1994), Reeves hadn't yet revived his career with *The*

Left: *Reluctant bride Freddie contemplates marriage to a gangland accountant in* Feeling Minnesota.

Matrix(1999). He'd recently turned down $11 million to make *Speed 2: Cruise Control* (1997), which proved a wise move. Reeves presumably agreed to audition for *Feeling Minnesota* on the assumption that a spell away from big-budget, high-pressure blockbuster movies would do him good. On the evidence of the finished film, it's a tricky call. In any event, Reeves' participation secured the necessary finance. With only three movies to her credit, Cameron Diaz wasn't yet a big enough name to attract backers.

Diaz described the production of *Feeling Minnesota* as both enjoyable and educational: "I've learned so much… I feel so fortunate to be a part of it." In contrast to Jim Carrey, Keanu Reeves had a real problem with his star status. As Diaz noted: "Jim is the kind of performer who thrives on the adulation of fans. Keanu, on the other hand, is terrified and embarrassed by it." Reeves' teenage fans soon tracked him down to the *Feeling Minnesota* location, making him very uneasy. Diaz could see that her co-star found this unwanted attention unsettling: "Every morning, there'd be dozens of little girls behind barriers across the street hoping to catch a glimpse of him…"

During the shoot, Cameron Diaz began a relationship with co-star Vincent D'Onofrio. While their affair proved short-lived, D'Onofrio taught Diaz a lot about the craft of film acting. As she explained to Louis B Hobson:

Vincent is the best acting coach I've ever had. He gave me confidence and taught me about approaching a character from the inside.

Diaz also met future boyfriend Matt Dillon, who was filming *Beautiful Girls* (1996) nearby. A former teen idol, Dillon had matured into a strong character actor. Staying at the same hotel as Dillon, Diaz immediately felt a strong connection between them. As both were romantically involved at the time, nothing came of this first encounter. A year later, things were different, as Diaz explained: "…it was instant attraction, so you could say it was love at second sight."

Co-producer Stacy Sher claimed that the characters in *Feeling Minnesota* are looking to "put together the broken pieces of their wrecked American Dream". This seems overblown and pretentious, yet contains a grain of truth. Sher also described the film as "a love story about two people who are afraid of falling in love", which is more accurate. Small-town girl Freddie (Diaz) is forced to marry dull accountant Sam (D'Onofrio) by his employer, club owner Red (Delroy Lindo). Offering patrons both arcade games and a strip joint, Red operates on the fringes of the law, paying out bribes to a sleazy cop (Aykroyd). In the event, Freddie is far more interested in Sam's footloose, ex-con brother Jjaks (Reeves). The new in-laws indulge in some intimate bonding at the wedding reception.

At this point, *Feeling Minnesota* looks like becoming a fugitive-lovers-on-the-run road movie. Without much of the road bit. Freddie is first seen running through urban wasteland in a wedding dress, hotly pursued by a car full of thugs. It's not clear exactly what she did for Red, though stripping seems a likely option. He claims that she ripped him off for a cool $10,000, a theft discovered by Sam, hence the

'arranged' marriage. Freddie disagrees, arguing that Red owed her the money. In the long run, it doesn't really matter.

Tough, foul-mouthed but not stupid, Freddie knocks back the beer at her sawn-off shotgun wedding, waiting for a chance to get the hell out. As Diaz sees it, Freddie is the film's true hero, "the smartest one out of all of them... so strong and just incredibly determined". To emphasise the character's downtrodden, wrong-side-of-the-tracks status, Diaz's naturally blonde hair was given a dyed look, complete with dark roots. Freddie looks believably pissed off most of the time. She's also fatalistic, informing Jjaks that "I'm dying. You're dying". Her homespun philosophy extends to "Time is like an orange", which leaves Jjaks understandably bemused.

Alone in a hostile world, Freddie has learned to be totally self-reliant, and now finds it almost impossible to trust or depend on anybody else. Freddie always takes the lead, pushing Jjaks to steal his brother's money for their new life together. Unlike Jjaks, Freddie still

believes in the American Dream, or at least her version of it. She wants to be a singing star in Las Vegas, driven by an idealised childhood memory of the ultra-tacky gambling Mecca. Sympathetic for most of the film, Freddie can seem manipulative and selfish, though director Steven Baigelman argued that she is just being practical. In Diaz's view, Freddie fights against her feelings for Jjaks, but is finally unable to resist "that crazy thing called love".

Feeling Minnesota loses its direction at the halfway mark, when Cameron Diaz's character disappears for a long, long stretch. The film badly misses her presence, which is a tribute to Diaz but makes for dull viewing. Even the black humour is laboured and unfunny. Brooding pretty-boy looks aside, Keanu Reeves isn't much of a screen performer. Jjaks is clearly intended as a character with Issues. Older brother Sam was always the favoured son, Jjaks' mother rejecting him at an early age. This may explain why Jjaks acts like he's in a permanently dazed state, passive and dim.

Discovering the motionless Freddie with

a large bullet hole in her side, Jjaks takes the body out into woodland for a DIY leaf burial. The local hospital might seem a better option but he's having memory problems and fears he may have killed her himself. Jjaks doesn't seem very shaken by Freddie's 'death', which both he and the audience are supposed to take for real. Diaz sees the Freddie-Jjaks relationship as crucial to the film: "I really think it's a love story." At times, the stars have a kind of wary, uneasy chemistry, but Reeves seems lost once the characters are required to reveal their true feelings. Reeves' best scene is Jjaks' first fight with Sam, a vicious, messy, non-graceful scrap. Sam bites off part of his brother's ear, which doesn't improve either of their moods.

After the lively start, with some mobile camerawork, *Feeling Minnesota* seems lacking in energy, with little dramatic or visual punch. Even the shoot-outs are dull. The supporting performances are similarly uneven. Having decided that both Sam and Jjaks have what he terms "crazy blood", D'Onofrio gives a very mannered, twitchy performance. At the time, Diaz described her co-star – and lover – as an "actor god". He seems less than divine here, Sam coming across as a sweaty, pig-faced jerk. Courtney Love is competent in a small role as a diner waitress, though her character doesn't get to participate in the action.

In truth, Diaz gives the film most of its vitality. Accompanied by the song 'Smoke Gets in Your Eyes', Freddie seduces Jjaks on his brother's bathroom floor, crying out "Bullseye!" when he hits the spot. A later fumble in Jjaks' (stolen) car releases the hand-brake. Neither of them seems too bothered as the car rolls down the road into a busy main street. With both

characters remaining fully clothed, these sex scenes are unusually frank and non-glamorised. Freddie complains more than once about Jjaks' abrasive stubble. She gives him an incentive blowjob by the side of a motel swimming pool, unconcerned about onlookers. At least this avoids severe facial chafing.

Diaz aside, *Feeling Minnesota* scores best with its quirky, throwaway details. Reeves' character should have been called 'Jack', but his utterly useless parents screwed up his birth certificate. Jjaks robs a gas station to pay for a wedding present, driving off in a stolen getaway vehicle. Brother Sam has truly awful dress sense, donning a light blue tuxedo and ruffled shirt for his wedding. No wonder Freddie wants to run. The outdoor wedding ceremony, staged on Sam's front lawn, is equally tacky, the guests shivering in the cold. In the hard realism department, Diaz sports a very convincing bullet wound. The eclectic soundtrack includes songs by Johnny Cash, Los Lobos, The Temptations, Nancy Sinatra, The Righteous Brothers and Bob Dylan. Minnesota is Dylan's home state, which might explain his less than cheery manner. Oddly, the film doesn't feature any songs by Soundgarden. Or Courtney Love.

Despite all the gloom, treachery, idiocy and general screw-ups, *Feeling Minnesota* signs off with a happy ending. Just when audiences think that Freddie has betrayed Jjaks for the hard cash she's pursued throughout the movie, her masterplan becomes clear. Jjaks catches up with her in the fabled Las Vegas, where Freddie now works as a topless dancer, except that Diaz is equipped with a bra and a large fan. Her fellow performers aren't so well covered. Reunited with Jjaks, Freddie gets the last line: "What took you so fucking long?" Good question.

Jersey Films and New Line opted to sell *Feeling Minnesota* on the back of the former's Quentin Tarantino hit: 'A twisted romance from the producers of *Pulp Fiction*'. Opening in the United States on Friday 13 September 1996 (unlucky for some), *Feeling Minnesota* earned only $3.1 million at the American box-office. Even popular critics Gene Siskel and Roger Ebert, who gave the film their 'Two Thumbs Up!' seal of approval, couldn't stir much audience interest.

Diaz reunited with New Line for the black comedy *Head Above Water* (1996). Like *Feeling Minnesota*, the film was made by the company's upmarket Fine Line division. Interviewed at the time, Diaz explained her reasons for accepting roles in low-budget, non-mainstream movie projects: "I just knew I wanted to carry on acting and to learn about acting. So I chose these smaller films."

Head Above Water is a remake of the Norwegian film *Hodet Over Vannet* (1993), directed by Nils Gaup. Hollywood has a reputation for taking successful foreign movies and redoing them very badly. Sadly, *Head Above Water* is not much of an exception, despite Diaz's best efforts.

The plot is pure farce, albeit of the grim kind. Taking an island vacation off the coast of Maine, reformed Party Girl Nathalie (Diaz) finds her life spinning seriously out of control when ex-boyfriend Kent Draper (Billy Zane) shows up and promptly dies on her. Discovering his corpse in the marital bed, Natalie feels that her much older husband George (Harvey Keitel), a Supreme Court judge, just won't understand.

With a better script and more inspired handling, *Head Above Water* could have been a great bad taste comedy along the lines of *There's Something About Mary*. The story offers jealousy, obsession, insanity and violent death. What a wasted opportunity. Director Jim Wilson, who also co-produced, has no sense of pace or timing, leaving his actors stranded. The film badly needs a little of the original's deadpan Scandinavian humour. Nathalie's amateurish attempts at corpse disposal should prompt some response in the audience, as she hides Kent's body in the cellar and dumps his clothes in the sea. George breaks the corpse's neck when he jumps on the cellar trapdoor, which is about as black as it comes.

With Kent soon out of the action, more or less, the film is essentially a three-hander. Nathalie must decide whether she can trust either George or Lance (Craig Sheffer), a close childhood friend who looks after their house. It soon becomes clear that she's the only remotely normal person around. Strolling around in unflattering shorts, George looks like a pipe-smoking klutz, as straight-laced as they come. In fact, Nathalie's husband is a control freak. He's the kind of man who keeps his quality delicatessen sausage in an old cigar box. We learn early on that George once squirted Kent with lighter fluid and threatened to burn him alive if he didn't leave Nathalie alone. This is not reasonable behaviour.

When Nathalie finally confesses all to George, he seems most concerned about the possible newspaper headlines: 'Nude ex-lover with broken neck delivered by jealous judge'. Safely offscreen, George beats up Kent's corpse, screaming "You wrecked my marriage!

Right: Coming up for
air in the disappointing
Head Above Water.

You wrecked my career! You wrecked my life!"
Not content with this post-mortem revenge,
he dismembers the body with a chainsaw and
hides the pieces in the freshly cemented steps
for a new gazebo. Once again, this should be
outrageous, shocking and strangely amusing.
It isn't. Harvey Keitel is one of Hollywood's
strongest character actors, memorably appearing in *Pulp Fiction* and *From Dusk Till Dawn*,
among many others. It says something about

Head Above Water that Keitel looks hopelessly
lost, giving a misguided performance that
verges on the inept.

Lance isn't much better than George,
despite his 'regular guy' appearance. He
repeatedly draws and sculpts Nathalie from
photographs, suggesting that his feelings for
her are not exactly platonic. Or wholesome.
Nathalie frolics underwater with Lance, hoping to distract him while George dumps

Kent's weighted body in the sea. The jaunty music suggests that this is supposed to be a great comic set-piece. Sadly not. At a crucial point, Lance believes George's version of events, not Nathalie's. This is the kind of movie where characters have to behave stupidly and illogically to keep the plot moving.

At the beginning of *Head Above Water*, Nathalie declares that "I've never really had much luck with men." Her odd relationship with George bears this out. In his professional capacity, George previously sentenced former substance abuser Nathalie to two years' probation. Nathalie claims to love George, yet he seems more like her guardian than her husband. While Lance and George go fishing, Nathalie sits in a deck-chair on the beach, restlessly turning the pages of *Vogue* magazine. Wearing sunglasses and a striped lemon-yellow swimsuit, she's all dressed up with nowhere to go. Clearly bored out of her mind, Nathalie regards Kent as a welcome, if risky diversion, a reminder of exciting times that now seem an eternity away. Still popping pills behind George's back, she can't disguise her guilty pleasure at seeing Kent again.

After what seems an eternity of twists, double-crosses and general arsing about, *Head Above Water* finally reaches some kind of climax. Trapped in the cellar by George to prevent her escape, Nathalie is finally forced to get assertive. Her initial fight back doesn't go to plan, Nathalie ending up with her feet in a tub of cement, poised to slide off the edge of a cliff. Making ingenious use of a shotgun and chainsaw, she finally escapes, leaving George impaled on his own gazebo. Frankly, he had it coming. As the sole survivor, Nathalie proves that she's finally beaten her drug dependency, showing determination, courage, resourcefulness and a strong will. Cameron Diaz embodies all these qualities with seemingly effortless assurance. All the more pity that she wasn't given a decent character to work with.

Head Above Water boasts one neat touch. Kent's postcard to Nathalie, mysteriously missing for most of the film, is of a Tex Avery-style wolf, a neat reference to both his predatory character and Diaz's earlier appearance in *The Mask*. The Phippsburg, Maine locations are easy on the eye and, if nothing else, the movie confirms everyone's worst suspicions about Supreme Court judges. New Line advertised their film with the slogan: 'Murder just became a water sport.' Nobody wanted to play. Distributed by Warner, *Head Above Water* was belatedly released on 25 June 1997 and rapidly sank without trace.

Despite this disappointment, Cameron Diaz's movie career continued to progress at an impressive rate. While most filmgoers hadn't seen much of her since *The Mask*, industry insiders regarded Diaz as a hot prospect for stardom. In 1996, she received the ShoWest Convention's annual award for Female Star of Tomorrow, chosen by the National Association of Theatre Owners (not to be confused with the other NATO). Previous winners included Nicole Kidman, Winona

Ryder and British actress Julia Ormond. Three out of four isn't bad.

Diaz's growing celebrity status was underlined with a guest appearance on the animated television series *Space Ghost Coast to Coast*. She played herself, or 'Herself', in the episode 'Surprise', first broadcast on 19 June 1996. Beginning in 1994, *Space Ghost* is as obscure as most of Cameron's early movies. It's pretty good, in a weird-funny kind of way, a deliberately low-tech superhero spoof. Retired costumed crimefighter Space Ghost stages a comeback as a late-night television talk show host, interviewing real-life celebrities via a television screen. Two years earlier, Jim Carrey and director Chuck Russell had plugged their new movie *The Mask* in an episode called, fittingly enough, 'The Mask'. For whatever reason, Cameron Diaz did not get to participate on that occasion. Other guests included Janeane Garofalo, Goldie Hawn, Mark Hamill, Michael Stipe, Bjork, Alice Cooper, Rob Zombie, Slash and Donny Osmond. Ben Stiller, shortly to co-star with Diaz in *There's Something About Mary*, also put in an appearance. For the record, 'Surprise' was the show's 27th episode.

Not many people have seen *Keys to Tulsa* (1997), and even fewer like it. Set in Tulsa, Oklahoma, this convoluted thriller centres on small-town, small-time film critic Richter Boudreau (Eric Stoltz), a character name more interesting than the character attached. Disowned by his wealthy family, Boudreau unwisely becomes involved with predatory ex-girlfriend Vicky Stover (Deborah Unger) and her drunken gun-freak brother Keith (Michael Rooker). There is a blackmail plot, initiated by Unger's loser husband Ronnie (James Spader),

exploiting the murder of a prostitute by the son of a local oil magnate. Aside from his amusing cameo role as a drug dealer in *Pulp Fiction*, Eric Stoltz has never enjoyed big Hollywood success and movies like this don't help.

Tenth-billed, Diaz only appears in the film's opening scene, as 'Trudy', Richter's blind date. Given approximately three minutes of screen time, Diaz contributes an assured, fun performance as a ditzy, spoiled rich kid. Her presence is sorely missed over the next 111 minutes, which seem like an eternity. Director Leslie Greif, who also co-produced, appears clueless about how to handle the material, and Harley Peyton's script is short on credible characters and even basic story. The film does have some amusingly over-the-top performances, notably from old hands Mary Tyler Moore and James Coburn. The muted finale suggests post-production tinkering. If it matters, *Keys to Tulsa* ran into problems with the US ratings boards, losing three minutes before it was granted a commercially acceptable 'R' rating. Released in the United States on 11 April 1997, the film picked up a rave review from trade journal *Variety*: "A wonderfully written and performed comic crime meller". It still flopped.

Three years and six movies into her acting career, Cameron Diaz had firmly established herself in a notoriously hard business. What she now needed was a high-profile vehicle to launch her back into the mainstream. *The Mask* would soon be ancient history, and a string of roles in quirky independent productions might only lead to more of the same. Having learned her craft and paid her dues, Diaz now wanted a taste of the big time. Even if it did mean singing very badly.

karaoke screaming

Three years on from *The Mask*, Cameron Diaz returned to mainstream Hollywood filmmaking with *My Best Friend's Wedding* (1997), starring Julia Roberts. Released by Columbia TriStar, the movie had a budget of $48 million, easily Diaz's most expensive film to date. Designed as a vehicle for Roberts, the film was effortlessly stolen from her by Diaz and British co-star Rupert Everett. There's also a very fine close-harmony, helium-enhanced rendition of 'Annie's Song'. John Denver may not have approved.

As well as reintroducing Cameron Diaz to the multiplex crowd, *My Best Friend's Wedding* was effectively a comeback film for Julia Roberts. Her previously glittering career had slumped badly during the mid-1990s with a series of flops, including *I Love Trouble* (1994), *Pret a Porter/Ready to Wear* (1994) and the much-delayed *Mary Reilly* (1996). Supporting performances in Neil Jordan's *Michael Collins* (1996) and Woody Allen's *Everyone Says I Love You* (1996) were well received, by and large, but Roberts needed to prove she could still score with a major starring role.

Diaz received third billing, after Roberts and leading man Dermot Mulroney. A prolific film actor, Mulroney tended to appear in small-scale independent productions, much as Diaz had done after *The Mask*. His relatively few big-budget movies included *Bad Girls* (1994), with Drew Barrymore, and *Copycat* (1995), with Sigourney Weaver, neither of which broke box-office records.

Australian director P J Hogan had scored an international hit with the dark comedy *Muriel's Wedding* (1994), whose Abba-fixated heroine was obsessed with marriage without knowing anything about love. Hogan recruited *Muriel* co-star Rachel Griffiths for his new movie, casting her as one of Diaz's sluttish country cousins.

My Best Friend's Wedding was largely filmed in and around Chicago, Illinois. Returning to high-profile, big-budget filmmaking after several years away proved a real eye-opener for Diaz. Julia Roberts' presence ensured that the tabloid press were out in force, hoping to get an exclusive picture that caught the star off-guard. Columbia put the production under tight security, closing the set to anyone without an official pass. Used to more relaxed working conditions, Diaz didn't envy Roberts' superstar status. According to Diaz, Roberts also worried about stalkers, which further restricted her movements away from the set. As Diaz explained to Louis B Hobson:

> I'm pretty positive I'd never want to be in the position Julia is in. It puts such restrictions on your personal and professional life... She is like an exotic plant that is only allowed to exist inside a protective shell... That's no life.

Interviewed mid-way through shooting on the film, Diaz heaped praise on Roberts: "I think she's incredibly beautiful... I love look-

Opposite: *Best of friends? Jules (Julia Roberts) and Kimmy in My Best Friend's Wedding.*

ing at her… She's just so damned gorgeous." Diaz also admired her co-star's working attitude, Roberts keeping the atmosphere cheerful and easygoing: "She tries so hard to keep everyone on set happy and laughing. She's a great jokester and she laughs a lot."

For her part, Roberts admired her co-star's energy and enthusiasm, describing Diaz as exuberant. Dermot Mulroney found Diaz's driving a little too exuberant, vowing never to get in a car with her again after one wild ride.

My Best Friend's Wedding is a comic variation on the old love triangle romance. Julia Roberts plays Julianne 'Jules' Potter, a successful New York food critic and author. About to hit the ripe old age of 28, Jules experiences an early mid-life crisis when an old friend, sportswriter Michael O'Neal (Mulroney), announces that he's getting married in a few days' time. Best buddies for nearly ten years, Jules and Mike were once a happy couple, until Jules suddenly ended the relationship. Afraid of closeness and commitment, she just couldn't handle the love of a good man. Or something along those lines. For all its merits, *My Best Friend's Wedding* isn't too strong on character motivation.

In order to sabotage the forthcoming wedding and 'win' Michael back, Jules must utterly discredit the bride, Kimberly Wallace (Diaz), known as Kim and Kimmy (close to Cami). Some critics accused the film of having an amoral tone, yet this is taking it too seriously. Discussing her scheming with George Downes (Everett), her gay friend and confidant, Jules claims that: "This is my whole life's happiness. I have to be ruthless." She sums it up better with the more snappy:

"George. She's toast." Rupert Everett is extremely good – elegant, witty and ingratiating – in a role that could have been a high-camp caricature. Most importantly, his scenes with Julia Roberts humanise her character, which would otherwise be seriously dislikeable. Everett's character proved so popular at test screenings, the producers shot additional scenes with the actor for the release version, including a new ending.

First seen waiting at the airport, Kimberly is a vision in a sleeveless, above-the-knee yellow dress. She nervously adjusts her hair and clothing, which look perfectly fine, her beaming smile revealing gleaming white teeth. She warmly embraces the startled Jules, a gesture which seems genuinely friendly rather than calculated for effect. Kim's billionaire father has organised a four-day wedding celebration, and she wants Jules to serve as her maid of honour.

An architecture student at the University of Chicago, Kim has little personal ambition beyond her marriage to Michael, or so she claims. It later becomes clear that she wants her own career, but will put it on hold to follow her new husband around the country's sports stadiums. Jules describes Kim as "bright-eyed and dreamy" and compares her to a creme brulée, "beautiful, sweet… irritatingly perfect". From a top food critic, it's probably a compliment. The two women discuss Michael's unusual snoring, both offering good imitations. Kim expertly recreates her fiancé's unusual phlegm rattle. She also drives recklessly fast and doesn't notice that Jules can't handle confined spaces, especially elevators. Very much a woman in love, Kim delivers the ultra-

Right: Celine takes it easy in A Life Less Ordinary.

naff line: "He's got you on a pedestal and me in his arms." At least it's heartfelt.

Jules first attempts to humiliate Kim with the Ordeal by Karaoke. Knowing that Kim can't sing a note, Jules takes her and Michael to the local singalong bar. Having rudely excluded Kim from the conversation, which Michael fails to notice, Jules forces her to take the microphone. Unable to back out, Kim delivers an incredibly flat, tone-deaf rendition of the Burt Bacharach-Dusty Springfield hit 'I Just Don't Know What To Do With Myself', complete with jarring feedback. Diaz captures Kim's embarrassment and sheer terror perfectly; the star claimed to be working from experience, having disabled a Karaoke machine with her off-key performance of Billy Joel's 'Big Shot'. Kim proves so game and spirited, however, that the initially hostile crowd gets behind her. Their vocal approval is echoed by Michael, Jules' wicked scheme backfiring 100 per cent. Diaz found shooting the sequence beneficial in at least one respect: "After the Karaoke scene in *My Best Friend's Wedding*, it's impossible to embarrass me." She later played

a similar scene in *Charlie's Angels*, her character's offbeat dancing winning over the hard-to-please Soul Train crowd.

Undaunted, Jules tries to turn the happy couple against each other, hatching an elaborate plot involving a bogus e-mail. The movie plays with the idea that Jules' cold-blooded scheming is in some ways a good thing. Shaken out of their romantic reverie, Michael and Kim are forced to confront the cracks beneath the surface of their seemingly perfect relationship. Perhaps these two Beautiful People are just not compatible. In one scene, Kim comes across as clinging, tearful and downright desperate. On the other hand, she's also shrewd at times, telling Jules: "You wouldn't be comfortable unless you were distinctive." It's arguable that Kim is getting a rough deal either way. Michael doesn't always seem that much of a catch, showing a boorish, insensitive side that isn't pleasant. He's also conveniently gullible, believing that the extremely gay George is Jules' new boyfriend. It seems odd, to say the least, that she hadn't mentioned his sexuality to 'best friend' Michael.

Kim is just too nice, or irritatingly perfect, to use strong language. Thankfully, the film doesn't cop out and have Jules and Kim suddenly turn into best buddies at the end. Jules may claim that "If I didn't have to hate her, I'd adore her", but it doesn't ring true.

My Best Friend's Wedding was released in the United States on 20 June 1997, opening in Britain two months later. One of the year's biggest hits, the film grossed $126 million at the American box-office, earning an additional $148 million overseas. The British release version removed all the stronger profanities, including Julia Roberts' "fuck", in order to secure a family-friendly PG rating. Diaz's appealing performance did not go unnoticed. In 1998, she received a Golden Satellite Award nomination for Best Performance by an Actress in a Supporting Role in a Motion Picture – Comedy or Musical. Even better, Diaz won her first Blockbuster Entertainment Award, for Favourite Supporting Actress – Comedy. The success of *My Best Friend's Wedding* also brought Diaz a higher level of recognition on the street. Interviewed by *Toronto Sun* reporter Bruce Kirkland, she seemed to take this in her stride:

> For two and a half years, everyone said: "Don't I know you? You look really familiar. Did we go to school together?" Then *My Best Friend's Wedding* came out and everyone said: "Oh, you're Cameron Diaz!" So that changed in a week.

A lot was expected from *A Life Less Ordinary* (1997), the first American-made film from the

As the wedding day draws near, Kim looks set to be an extremely unlucky bride. Once Jules' treachery is revealed, Kim finally gets mad at her, in the unusual setting of a women's restroom. Diaz completely outguns Roberts in this scene, Kim informing her duplicitous new 'friend' that she's a "...two-faced, big-haired food critic." Even in a rage,

Above: *Celine Naville, millionaire's daughter and kidnap victim in A Life Less Ordinary.*

British team of producer Andrew Macdonald, director Danny Boyle, writer John Hodge and leading man Ewan McGregor. As the eagerly awaited follow-up to the hits *Shallow Grave* (1994) and *Trainspotting* (1995), the movie had to deliver in a big way. In the event, *A Life Less Ordinary* proved a case of third time unlucky. The odd, pretentious title didn't get things off to the best start, and both critics and fans regarded the movie as a major disappointment. It's certainly a mess, filled with more ideas, plot strands and general weirdness than it can handle.

Produced by Polygram and Britain's Channel 4, *A Life Less Ordinary* had a modest $12 million budget. Diaz agreed to take the second-billed, co-starring role of Celine Naville, a millionaire's daughter who more or less stages her own kidnapping. McGregor and Diaz were backed by a strong supporting cast, including Holly Hunter, *Feeling Minnesota* co-star Delroy Lindo and British actor Ian Holm. The stars got on extremely well during shooting, their good working relationship reflected in the finished film. Diaz felt that the screen chemistry between her and McGregor was the best she'd yet experienced: "We laughed for two months solid. Ewan is a remarkable talent. Everything he does for the camera is so truthful and believable." Director Danny Boyle felt that both Diaz and McGregor benefited from strong family backgrounds:

I think part of the reason Cameron and Ewan hit it off so well is that they both come from close families. They're both loved, and very centred.

Above: *All tied up and nowhere to go in* A Life Less Ordinary.

Opening in an ultra-white, ultra-bright version of Heaven, *A Life Less Ordinary* is mostly set in Utah. Spoiled rich girl Celine swims on her back in a deluxe open-air pool. Her fetching black costume permits director Boyle some choice shots of Diaz's cleavage. Despite the trappings of vast wealth, Celine is clearly bored rigid, shooting apples off her butler's head for fun. Meanwhile, down at the other end of the social spectrum, humble menial worker Robert Lewis (McGregor) is having a very bad day. Fired from his cleaning job by his boss, Celine's father (Holm), he is also dumped by his girlfriend for her aerobics teacher. Looking for revenge on Mr Naville, Robert ends up subjecting willing 'victim' Celine to one of the least competent kidnappings of all time, obliging her to take charge of the operation.

Burdened by half-assed symbolism and a smart-ass script, the film is often misjudged and downright confusing. Two trainee angels (Hunter and Lindo) are ordered to bring Celine and Robert together in true love. Decked out with peroxide hair, Holly Hunter gives a self-consciously kooky, kittenish performance that becomes embarrassing to watch. Most viewers will cheer when Diaz

she easily beats him in a drinking game. Acting like a prototype Naked Chef, Robert cooks dinner for Celine, only to discover that she won't eat red meat or non free-range eggs, on moral grounds. He could have checked.

Celine reveals that she was kidnapped once before, at the age of 12. Her father took six weeks to pay up, which suggests a seriously dysfunctional relationship. Forced to teach Robert the basics of kidnapping, Celine instructs him on how to make a threatening telephone call. Crammed into a phone booth, Diaz and McGregor have a great interplay here, suggesting what the movie could have been without the crass fantasy element. After a hard day's instruction, Celine remains unimpressed: "You are the worst kidnapper I've ever met." Robert doesn't even know how much ransom to demand, Celine assuring him that "Half a million dollars is not a lot of money for a woman like me." This could sound arrogant, yet Celine is fully aware of her market value. Aiming to get back at her cold, unpleasant father, Celine wants to bleed him dry. Speaking of which, she cuts her own arm with a razor, requiring the blood for a suitably scary ransom note. It comes as no surprise when Robert faints dead away at the sight.

Unfortunately, the film's jokey kidnapping angle goes badly awry at one point, the humour evaporating in a blaze of bad taste. Celine decides to rob a bank after her father cancels her credit card. Pointing a loaded gun at a terrified teenage girl's head, Celine threatens to kill her. There is nothing remotely funny about this scene, which the actors play dead straight, resuming the light-hearted comedy in the next sequence without a beat.

punches her in the face. The diminutive Ian Holm isn't too believable as the statuesque Diaz's father, and his on-off American accent doesn't help the plausibility factor.

Diaz gives a spirited performance throughout the film, handling the comedy bullshitting especially well. Celine is stronger, smarter, more assertive and more confident than the generally useless Robert. Quickly escaping from her bonds, she chops firewood while he reads a trashy novel. At the local bar,

Above: With Life Less Ordinary co-star Ewan McGregor.

Bad idea. Celine sees the whole caper as a big adventure, turned on by her new life of crime: "I'm having a *great* time."

Aside from an awful pair of black and white striped gloves, Diaz at least gets a decent wardrobe, courtesy of Gianni Versace. She looks especially good in black, the camera lingering on her high-class underwear. At one point, Celine takes part in a bizarre photo shoot, the kind of modelling assignment that the 16-year-old Cameron Diaz would have turned down. In debt to her crazed ex-boyfriend (Stanley Tucci), a dentist to the rich and famous, Celine allows him to photograph her in a long blonde wig and white tunic. It's a weird scene that just comes and goes to no great purpose. Perhaps someone told scriptwriter John Hodge to increase the wacky factor. Ewan McGregor is outfitted by Gucci, which Robert presumably paid for on his cleaner's wage. Pity they couldn't do anything about his hair.

Celine and Robert finally start to bond during a Country and Western Karaoke session. Displaying a much better (dubbed?) singing voice than she did in *My Best Friend's Wedding*, Diaz performs a duet with McGregor, which turns into an impressive dance routine. The sequence eventually spins off into outright fantasy, further proof that the filmmakers didn't have enough faith in their leading characters. At times, the script seems uncertain where to go next. Robert's ambition to become a pulp novelist doesn't really lead anywhere. A subplot involving Celine's mother, cruelly discarded by Mr Naville, is similarly undeveloped.

As with a number of Diaz's characters, there is a suggestion that Celine is afraid of love, if little else. She stays cool even when gagged and bound with cheap-looking orange rope. To date, Diaz has been tied up in *The Mask*, *Head Above Water*, *A Life Less Ordinary* and *Being John Malkovich*. Is this a thinly veiled bondage fantasy or just a time-honoured dramatic device? In *A Life Less Ordinary*, she is also blindfolded for much of the climax, then locked in the trunk of a car, a double insult for a character who can't even drive. At long last, Celine rescues Robert from her father, finally putting her sharp-shooting skills to good use.

As the closing credits roll, stop-motion puppet versions of Robert and Celine retrieve a bag full of ransom money and move to a castle in Scotland. This second-rate excursion into Wallace and Gromit territory makes little sense, not that there was much of it beforehand. The Cameron Diaz puppet doesn't even do her justice. The 'non-stop pop hits' soundtrack has something for just about everyone: Diana Ross and the Supremes, Elvis Presley, Underworld, Elastica, The Shirelles, The Prodigy, Orbital, Beck, REM, Ash and Oasis. For the geographically inclined, the Utah locations, including Salt Lake City, are striking.

A Life Less Ordinary opened in America on 26 October 1997. The $4.3 million US gross was matched by around $5 million elsewhere, a total that didn't even cover the production budget. In Britain, *Time Out* reviewer Tom Charity praised Diaz's spirited performance: "a real livewire who jump starts the movie more than once". Despite the disappointing box-office and mixed reviews, Diaz remained loyal to *A Life Less Ordinary*. She later suggest-

ed that the nationwide, 1200-screen release of the film in the US was a mistake. *A Life Less Ordinary* could have done much better with a low-key release, slowly building an audience by word of mouth. By way of compensation, Diaz and McGregor shared a 1998 MTV Movie Award nomination for Best Dance Sequence. They didn't win.

Fear and Loathing in Las Vegas (1998) is one of those movies that may be dug up in 50 years and proclaimed as a neglected masterpiece. For the time being, however, most viewers will agree that it sucks. Diaz makes a brief appearance in this tedious, drugged-out odyssey as 'Blonde TV Reporter'. The film was directed and co-written by *Monty Python* veteran Terry Gilliam, presumably the main reason *Python* fan Diaz took part. A gifted filmmaker with an extraordinary visual imagination, Gilliam came hopelessly unstuck on this occasion.

Based on the cult 1972 book by Hunter S Thompson, *Fear and Loathing* follows the adventures of journalist Raoul Duke (Johnny Depp) and his attorney Dr Gonzo (Benicio Del Toro). Fans of the film claim that the 1971-set story is really about the Vietnam protest movement and the death of 1960s idealism. The substance-abusing Raoul and Gonzo behave insanely because the world around them is insane. Maybe so, but they still look like two obnoxious jerks with nightmare Hawaiian shirts and bad hair. On the plus side, both men do amusing walks.

At the time, Gilliam needed to find a new film project after failing to get *The Defective Detective* off the ground, despite interest from Bruce Willis and Nicholas Cage. Johnny Depp was already involved with the *Fear and Loathing* movie, produced by Rhino Films for distribution through Universal.

Diaz happened to be in London with her business manager, who told Gilliam about the project. The original writer-director, Alex Cox, had recently been fired from the production. Taking on the job, Gilliam wrote a new script, with Tony Grisoni, in ten days.

Gilliam tried to shoot *Fear and Loathing* for a bargain $12 million, though the film ended up costing $18.5 million. He reportedly disliked the executives at Rhino Films, accusing them of playing games, threatening to reinstate Alex Cox whenever he argued. The director particularly disliked novice producer Steve Nemeth, and the two failed to see eye to eye during filming. For whatever reason, *Fear and Loathing* began production before the final contracts were drawn up, Gilliam later alleging that Rhino Films reneged on his original agreed fee. Despite these problems, shooting was completed in just 55 days.

For all the hard work and dedication put into *Fear and Loathing in Las Vegas*, the film misfires from the start. Johnny Depp's Raoul Duke is supposedly covering the Mint 400 Desert Race, one of the top motorcycle events. His drug-blitzed mind is elsewhere, in a land of hallucinatory bats, human-sized lounge lizards, a coiffured dwarf and an angel with a flaming sword. Half of the time, it's near impossible to make out what Duke is saying, rendering the frequent voice-over more frustrating than illuminating. Benicio Del Toro put on 40 pounds for his role, along with a hairstyle from Hell. While one brief scene shows that Dr Gonzo is a real lawyer, heavily involved with the Civil Rights movement, he still comes across as a repellent slob with a nasty violent streak.

Gilliam seems uncertain about what he wanted to do with the film. He has described it as taking a moral stance, drawing parallels between Las Vegas' gaudy carnival of greed and Dante's *Inferno*. At the same time, he wanted to be non-apologetic about Raoul and Gonzo's drug-fuelled rampage, which leaves at least one character in a state of terror. On the other hand, *Fear and Loathing* is an anti-drug film, or at least honest about the highs and lows of drug use. The film rightly attacks Nevada's absurdly harsh anti-drug laws of the early 1970s: 20 years for possession of marijuana and a life sentence for dealing. But in terms of entertainment, the best moment comes when Raoul hits Gonzo on the head with a grapefruit.

The chance to work with Terry Gilliam and Johnny Depp on such a cult property attracted a number of well-known actors and musicians. As well as Cameron Diaz, there are cameos from Lyle Lovett, Gary Busey, Ellen Barkin, Penn Gillette, Harry Dean Stanton and Christina Ricci, who plays a teenage runaway with a Barbra Streisand fixation.

Diaz's television journalist appears in one short scene, stuck in an elevator with Raoul and Gonzo. As the latter is mumbling incomprehensibly and wielding a pocket knife, she looks understandably uncomfortable. Diaz is dressed in an authentic period white and brown outfit, with puffed sleeves and a very 1970s big collar. Her hair is done-up bouffant-style, held in place with an Alice band. This may, or may not, be one of the movie's various *Alice in Wonderland* references, which include the Jefferson Airplane hit 'White Rabbit'. Diaz's character mistakes Dr Gonzo for one of the competing motorcyclists, leading the stoned Gonzo to fantasise that she loves him. Not a good thought.

Terry Gilliam described *Fear and Loathing in Las Vegas* as "a cinematic enema for the nineties". Critics and audiences soon told him where to stick it, however. Released in the United States on 25 May 1998, *Fear and Loathing* made only $10.5 million during its North American theatrical run. Gilliam claims that the film later became a cult hit with American teenagers, on the grounds of its 'honesty'.

Less than a month after *Fear and Loathing*'s box-office flop, Diaz reappeared on American cinema screens in a film that proved a lot more popular. Distributed by Twentieth Century Fox, *There's Something About Mary* (1998) gave Diaz her break-through, career-defining role. Mary Jensen Matthews may not be her most interesting or dominant character, yet the combination of beauty, decency and a working knowledge of sex toys struck a chord with audiences.

There's Something About Mary is not a perfect film by any means. It's too long, there are slow stretches between the comedy high-lights, and the ending is a bit lame. On the other hand, it is extremely funny. The movie sprang from the inventive comic minds of the Farrelly Brothers, Peter and Bobby. Never too interested in wit, subtlety or character devel-opment, the Farrellys had achieved major Hollywood success with a distinctive brand of gross-out slapstick. Their debut movie, New Line's *Dumb and Dumber* (1994), made $117 million in the US on a $15 million budget, half of which was Jim Carrey's star salary. The follow-up, *Kingpin* (1996), did just as well,

though the sleazy, low-life characters proved too gross for more sensitive audiences.

Despite this success, *There's Something About Mary* was budgeted at a modest $23 mil-lion, half the cost of *My Best Friend's Wedding*. The Farrellys badly wanted Cameron Diaz to play Mary, regarding her as their first and only choice. They even delayed the film's start date to fit in with Diaz's busy schedule. Diaz's initial reaction to the script was not entirely favourable, as she explained to Louis B Hobson:

> **I definitely had serious qualms about certain scenes, but the Farrellys kept assuring me they'd play funny on screen. They kept telling me it was meant to be a cross between *When Harry Met Sally* and *Blazing Saddles*. I had to put my faith in that promise...**

Her biggest problem with the screenplay was a nude scene, which seemed included merely for gratuitous titillation: "I though it was sleazy and exploitative given that this was just a slap-stick comedy." Having been duped into posing naked during her early modelling days, Diaz was not about to disrobe for a cheap thrill. Once her feelings were known, the Farrellys immediately agreed to drop the idea. "I said no and there was no discussion, which I really respected." In the event, the Farrellys turned the whole nudity issue into yet another of the movie's gross-out jokes. While some of Diaz's fans may have been disappointed, most would agree that her decision was right. "I just didn't want Mary or myself to become an object of ridicule." Before signing up for the film, Diaz showed the script to her mother, who liked

what she read: "…she just howled. She was the one who said I absolutely had to do it."

Top-billed for the first time since *The Last Supper*, Diaz received a $2 million fee for *There's Something About Mary*, a reflection of her rising star status. While major league Hollywood players like John Travolta supposedly earned ten times that amount, Diaz would soon catch up. A mere three years later, she was paid $15 million for her starring role in *The Sweetest Thing* (2002).

Diaz's co-stars on *There's Something About Mary* included television comedian Ben Stiller, top British comic Lee Evans and Matt Dillon. At the time, Diaz was romantically involved with Dillon, though the Farrellys were supposedly unaware of this. As Diaz explained: "They never read gossip magazines or the trade papers." In fairness, Dillon had wanted to keep the relationship private, out of the media spotlight. Diaz found this hard to deal with and persuaded Dillon to go public:

> **I can't keep a secret, especially when I'm happy. I haven't had many relationships so I want people to know when I'm in such a great one.**

As it happened, Diaz and Dillon had already thought about working together. Interviewed by *Toronto Sun* reporter Jim Slotek in October 1997, Diaz revealed:

> **We're looking for something to do together… It's got to be the right thing, really, especially if you're in a relationship. It doesn't need that kind of pressure.**

Above: *Dreamgirl Mary Jensen in There's Something About Mary.*

Initially, Diaz didn't think that *Mary* was the ideal project for their first co-starring venture. The Farrellys wanted Dillon to play the role of a sleazy private detective, which she considered bad casting:

> **I told them I thought Matt was too good-looking to play such a loser. They told me that wouldn't be a problem considering what they had in store for that character. Matt was such a great sport to let them make him look so silly.**

Above: With big sister Chimene at the premiere of There's Something About Mary.

monitoring the action on video screens. Dia[z] had no problem with this unorthodox div[i]sion of directing duties, explaining: "It's rea[l]ly interesting the way they worked togethe[r] There was no competitiveness. They worke[d] totally harmoniously…"

For their part, the Farrellys never doub[t]ed that they'd made the right choice for Mar[y]. As Peter Farrelly later explained: "Cameron [is] Mary. Like Mary, Cameron seems like th[e] ultimate woman. Every guy on the set wa[s] crazy about her." Bobby Farrelly echoed th[e] sentiment: "She's beautiful, sweet, fun an[d] nice." Diaz succumbed to helpless laught[er] filming one scene with Lin Shaye, who playe[d] Mary's man-crazed neighbour Magda, an[d] Puffy the dog. Called upon to lick Shaye['s] face, Puffy liked the taste of her make-up an[d] wouldn't stop the fast-tongue action. Di[az] also liked the Miami locations, subsequent[ly] acquiring a restaurant, Bambu, in the city.

Working with real-life boyfriend Ma[tt] Dillon also proved good fun. As Diaz explaine[d]

It was a great experience. The fact [that] we're still together and happier than ever says it all… We were surprised ourselves that spending that much time together every day was so rewarding. People told us that much togetherness could get ugly. It didn't.

Diaz and Dillon enjoyed their first screen c[ol]laboration so much, they announced plans [for] a second film together. "The next one will [be] a little less broad. I can promise you tha[t]." Sadly, it was not to be.

There's Something About Mary is a tale

Cameron also recruited her father to play a small role in the film. Emilio Diaz can be glimpsed as one of the jailbirds who keep Ben Stiller's character company during a *very* bad night. The Farrellys also wanted Diaz's mother, who'd approved their script, to make a cameo appearance. Sadly, Cameron couldn't persuade her; "she chickened out".

There's Something About Mary was filmed over ten weeks, with location shooting in Rhode Island and Miami, Florida. Peter Farrelly worked on set with the actors, while Bobby Farrelly stayed behind the cameras,

frustrated love that borders on obsession. Back in the distant days of 1985, Rhode Island high school student Ted Stroehmann (Stiller) has a mad crush on Mary. He also has dental braces, bad hair and worse clothes. Mary is first seen riding along on her push bike, hair flowing, pretty in pink, waving to her many friends. The harsh high school rulebook dictates that she's a winner, he's a loser and they'll stay worlds apart. Through an unlikely set of circumstances, Ted ends up as Mary's prom date. After an equally bizarre accident, he is carried off on a stretcher before they've even left her house. Thirteen unlucky years later, Ted is still hung up on Mary and vows to track her down. Despite having better dress sense, he is still a put-upon loser.

One unusual aspect of *There's Something About Mary* is the music, which directly comments on the story. There are linking songs written and performed by Jonathan Richman, who appears onscreen, sitting in a tree and selling hot dogs. The big selling point, of course, is the Farrellys' trademark bad taste humour. As Cameron Diaz put it:

They cross every line in this movie, which is outrageous and totally unique. The thing you learn very quickly with Peter and Bobby is that you can never go too far.

In *There's Something About Mary*, the Farrellys turn gross comedy into some kind of art form, humiliating their characters to the nth degree. There are jokes about the Japanese, people in wheelchairs, homosexuals, bad modern movies and animal cruelty. One of the film's

running gags will probably be lost on many of the target audience. Mary's favourite movie is the cult black comedy *Harold and Maude* (1971), which she describes as "one of the greatest love stories of all time". The film's plot, never mentioned in *Mary*, revolves around an unusual love affair between a death-obsessed 20-year-old man and an 80-year-old woman. It's strangely touching.

Most of the big laughs in *There's Something About Mary* centre on Ted's numerous misadventures as he pursues his dream woman. Arrested during a police raid on a gay pick-up spot, Ted is rapidly accused of being a serial killer. The other main victim is Puffy the dog, who undergoes doping, electrocution and burning, all in one evening. He later overdoses on speed, which does nothing for his temperament, and ends up flying through a closed window. Encased in a full body cast, Puffy is at least protected from further harm.

The notorious zipper scene is probably the most excruciating, for male viewers at any rate. Near the start of the film, a nervous Ted visits the bathroom while Mary gets ready for the high school prom. With his mind on other things, he doesn't pay attention when he is zipping up. There is a mercifully brief shot of Ted's trapped penis, which could still traumatise more sensitive minds. Two weeks in hospital seems a small price to pay for fully restored genitals. Not that the movie dwells on this point. Thirteen years on, Ted's manhood gets him into trouble again. Having finally secured another date with Mary, he is convinced by a supposed friend that a little hand relief will clear his mind. The sound effects alone are truly cringe-making. This, of course, leads to the celebrated 'hair gel' scene, where Mary sees a whitish substance hanging from Ted's left earlobe and reaches the wrong conclusion.

For the penile *pièce de résistance*, Ted is bitten in the crotch by Puffy, spinning around in agony. By comparison, a hook in the mouth during a fishing trip seems like nothing. This relentless barrage of pain and humiliation won Diaz's approval: "I think nearly every joke in here I find funny. Actually, I can't think of any I didn't think was funny."

The kind-hearted, well-intentioned Ted is invariably misunderstood, his good deeds resented. Most of the characters he meets are borderline crazy, though only one turns out to be a murderer. High-profile professionals such as cops, firemen, ambulance crews and psychiatrists are revealed as incompetent, useless jerks. Even Mary's parents seem a little weird, gazing at Ted's ensnared groin with horrified fascination. Sympathy is in short supply round these parts, though Mary's stepfather (Keith David) takes the trouble to ask: "Is it the frank or the beans?"

By contrast, Mary is sensitive and compassionate, and sees these qualities in Ted where others only see a champion schmuck. Wearing a striking blue dress for the abortive prom date, Mary remains an unattainable vision in Ted's tortured mind. The Carpenters hit '(They Long To Be) Close to You' is heard during the zipper sequence, a taunting reminder that Ted was briefly so near to the woman of his dreams. Still a friend to all years later, Mary works with the handicapped and likes her cooked meat on a stick. A sports fanatic, much like Cameron Diaz, she attends baseball games, drives mini racing cars and

swings a mean golf club. She's not coy about sexual relationships, casually dismissing a recent break-up: "I've got a vibrator." Unconcerned with money or status, Mary has very definite ideas regarding love, which is about "two people connecting, having something in common, you know, kindred spirits".

While Mary strolls around her apartment in white underwear, the film gleefully undermines male viewer expectations of nudity, cutting to Magda's less alluring body at the last minute. It's notable that the Farrellys always have Diaz play her role completely seriously. As the star pointed out: "I'm essentially the straight man in this movie. It's the guys who get to do all the wild and bizarre stuff." Even when she's rubbing Ted's sperm into her hair, Mary remains the calm centre for the other character's demented antics. Frankly, the stick-up 'quiff' look doesn't suit her. Trusting to the point of naïveté, she is close friends with Norman Phipps (Evans), a pizza delivery boy who poses as a disabled British architect on crutches. Mary even becomes attracted to sleazy private investigator Pat Healy (Dillon), despite his very dodgy moustache. Following Mary through town and bugging her apartment, Healy exploits her image of the ideal man.

For all its deliberate grossness and bad taste, *There's Something About Mary* is a moral, even sentimental film. This is particularly evident in the depiction of Mary's mentally handicapped brother, Warren (W Earl Brown), who weighs in at a hefty 230 pounds and enjoys piggy-back rides. While a number of scum characters play cruel tricks on Warren, the film always treats him as a sym-

pathetic character, rather than the butt of jokes. The idea of obsessive desire touches on the theme of stalking, Mary having changed her name to shake off an unwelcome admirer. Ted foolishly hires the sneaky private eye to do his initial surveillance, only for the latter to fixate on Mary himself. Chastened, Ted concludes that "I'm no better than any of these guys", though audiences – and Mary – know better. Lust is a strong, dangerous thing and men will trample each other to death in their pursuit of a desirable female. Phipps even had a friend break his back with a base-ball bat in order to meet Mary, a physiothera-pist. While some would say Diaz is well worth it, there are limits. Faced with five possible suitors, Mary has only one reasonable choice as far as audiences are concerned.

There's Something About Mary's most famous publicity shot features Cameron Diaz in a pink mini-dress and sandals, leaning for-ward on her left knee, her hair running across the right side of her face. This image sums up Mary to a tee: attractive, open and friendly. The film's tagline took a very different approach: 'Be Offended. Be *Very* Offended.' Released in the United States on 19 July 1998, *There's Something About Mary* quickly became the film event of the year, at least in the gross-out comedy stakes. The movie's impressive $176.5 million domestic gross was matched by a $140 million box-office take overseas, $15.6 million of which came from the UK.

While *There's Something About Mary* never looked like obvious Academy Award material, Cameron Diaz enjoyed major recog-nition for her contribution to the film. In 1999, she received an ALMA Award nomina-

Above: *The infamous 'hair gel' shot from* There's Something About Mary.

tion for Outstanding Actress in a Feature Film in a Crossover Role, and a Golden Globe nom-ination for Best Performance by an Actress in a Motion Picture – Comedy/Musical. The MTV Movie Awards nominated her for Best Comedic Performance, Best Kiss and Best On-Screen Duo, the last two shared with co-star Ben Stiller. Even better, Diaz won the New York Film Critics Circle Award for Best Actress, the Blockbuster Entertainment Award for Favorite Actress – Comedy, the MTV Movie Award for Best Female Performance, and the American Comedy Award for Funniest Actress in a Motion Picture (Leading Role). Not a bad haul.

There's Something About Mary rapidly established itself as a true comedy classic. The American Film Institute included *Mary* in its epic television documentary *AFI's 100 Years, 100 Laughs: America's Funniest Movies* (2000). Diaz made a brief appearance, discussing the movie and her role in it.

head trips

From black comedy of the grossly funny kind to blacker comedy of the grim, nasty kind. Even with her new star status, Cameron Diaz could not save *Very Bad Things* (1998) from critical and box-office oblivion. It's tempting to dismiss the movie as simply a Very Bad Film, yet there are hints here and there of what could have been.

Making his big screen debut as a writer-director, actor Peter Berg showed both imagination and a very dark sense of humour. Starting off with the bachelor party from Hell, the film plunges into the lowest depths of human wretchedness without a safety net. What *Chicago Hope* veteran Berg couldn't do was make the events funny, even in a ghastly, cringing kind of way. *Very Bad Things* is one of those movies where the intriguing premise is screwed up by the execution. The characters are unsympathetic, the plot becomes increasingly ludicrous, and the overall film has no sense of style or tone. As *Charlie's Angels* later demonstrated, you can get away with a lot if you know what you're doing.

Despite his lack of experience, Peter Berg secured both a $10 million budget and a distribution deal from Universal. Leading man Christian Slater also served as one of the film's executive producers, which probably helped. Slater plays shifty real estate dealer Robert Boyd, who organises a Las Vegas stag night for his good buddy Kyle 'Fish' Fisher (Jon Favreau). Second billed to Slater, Diaz took the role of Laura Garrety, the bride-to-be who knows what she wants and will let nothing stand in her way. The script involved Diaz going through yet another screen wedding, her fourth in quick succession. Nevertheless,

she liked what she read: "It's very dark and very cynical and therefore very funny."

The supporting cast originally included *Saturday Night Live* comic Adam Sandler, who dropped out before shooting began to star in *The Waterboy* (1998), which he also co-wrote. A more light-hearted comedy, *The Waterboy* proved a surprise hit in the United States, launching Sandler's film career. *Very Bad Things* didn't get so lucky. Sandler was replaced by Jeremy Piven, who'd given a strong performance in *Grosse Pointe Blank* (1997), another black comedy, but seems badly miscast here.

Throughout *Very Bad Things*, the deliberate bad taste and apparent amorality are utterly ineffective. The stag night sequence sets the depressing tone. It quickly becomes clear that these particular party animals are Grade A arseholes. Gambling, boozing and coke-snorting aside, they behave like jerks all the time: loud, arrogant and two-faced. The stripper hired for the occasion turns out to be a prostitute. She's accidentally killed – via a coat peg through the back of her skull – while having rampant sex with the Piven character, who turns necrophile without even knowing it. Adam Sandler probably didn't need this kind of role on his CV. Faced with a "105-pound problem", not to mention a trashed hotel room full of illicit substances, the ice-cold Boyd talks the others into secretly dumping the corpse. The police have got better things to do with their time than worry about a missing low-rent hooker.

This exercise in damage limitation leads to bribes, clean-ups, corpse dismemberment and murder. Peter Berg's script plays with male

Opposite: *A lighter moment for Laura in* Very Bad Things. *It won't last long.*

Left: *Taking direction from Peter Berg during the filming of* Very Bad Things.

bonding, group loyalty and peer pressure, before switching to guilt, suspicion, paranoia and mental breakdown. Berg's direction is over-reliant on restless, off-centre camerawork and music video-style visuals. Throughout the whole weary business, Laura's intended seems no better than his buddies. While Fish draws the line at actual sex with their oriental 'hostess', he's happy to have her writhe naked in his face, big-time. It doesn't help that co-star Jon Favreau looks like a shaved gorilla, only without the cute animal appeal.

Leading man Christian Slater is utterly charmless in a pivotal role. Boyd should be a seductive demonic force, leading his 'friends' down the blood-slicked path of damnation. Slater has often been accused of giving second-rate Jack Nicholson impersonations instead of actual performances. On this occasion, he's guilty as hell, smirking and gesticulating to irritating effect. Boyd seems to embody the dark side of self-help therapy and personal empowerment, coming out with lines like: "Love does not lose." The most sympathetic character is an increasingly suspicious wife (Jeanne Tripplehorn), if only because she won't take any of Boyd's smooth-talking bullshit.

Decked out in some of the least flattering costumes of her career, Diaz deserved better than this. Laura Garrety spends most of her screen time reacting to events she doesn't understand. After the initial fun and games in Las Vegas, Laura asks Fish if he snorted any cocaine ("You sound a little funny, honey"), without seeming too bothered by the idea. Laura feels that her fiancé should 're-evaluate' some of his long-term friendships. This has less to do with her sound judgment than the fact that she's a monster control freak. Laura is fixated on the gold-trim padded seats she wants for the wedding, not to mention the high cost of mobile phone calls. She has model tables and chairs to work out the seating plan for the wedding reception and even organises a dress rehearsal for the dinner.

Laura's obsession with every last detail of the ceremony is made to seem even more petty when contrasted with the terrible events involving her husband-to-be. She soon comes across as nagging, intolerant, paranoid and deeply insecure. Statements such as "I am a creature like no other" do not endear her to anyone. If Laura seems a little slow to twig that things are not good, it's because she just doesn't care. When Fish finally confesses all, Laura's reaction shows that she's even crazier than the others. She's spent 27 years waiting for her wedding, focusing and preparing for the marriage ceremony, and a few deaths are of no importance.

Diaz does eventually get to participate in the action, beating Slater's head to a pulp with a coat-stand. Staring down at the bloody mess, she looks elated. Hit him one more time for us, Cameron. Wiping the sweat from her armpits, Laura orders Fish to kill his last surviving friend, the only witness left. Diaz shows a real flair for this crazed ruthlessness and the film seems poised to hit the right gear at long last. Unfortunately, it's about ten minutes from the end.

Looking for the ultimate feel-bad ending, *Very Bad Things* pulls out all the stops. Following a car smash, Fish ends up as a double amputee in a wheelchair. Laura is now a drudge-slave housewife, forced to look after both her husband and two bratty kids belonging to his dead friend. So much for her dream of a perfect marriage. Wearing rubber gloves, clutching cleaning fluid and a brush, she looks truly insane. The final shot of the movie sees Laura lying in the middle of a road, screaming her head off. Maybe there is a God, after all. The closing credits are accompanied by Limp Bizkit's demented, heavy rock version of the George Michael classic 'Faith'. It's the best bit in the film.

Out on the publicity trail, Cameron

Diaz made it clear that *Very Bad Things* was not another cheery comedy: "I don't think it is something that is for everyone. Definitely not for everyone." Or anyone, as it turned out. Marketed with the tagline 'They've Been Bad. Very Bad', *Very Bad Things* hit US cinemas on 29 November 1998. Forewarned by some hostile reviews, audiences didn't like what they saw, and the film made only $9.8 million in its home territory. Released in Britain on 31 January 1999, the movie grossed an unimpressive £1.8 million. It's been claimed that the film improves immensely on a second viewing. This may well be true, yet it's difficult to imagine many viewers wanting to find out.

Man Woman Film (1999) is probably the oddest movie in the Cameron Diaz filmography, and also the most difficult to track down. It's never received a theatrical release in any country, and isn't likely to hit the shelves of Blockbuster anytime soon. Written and directed by UCLA graduate Cameron Pearson, the film cost all of $35,000. All of which prompts the question: what was Diaz, a major Hollywood star, doing in a no-budget student film that almost no one would ever see? In fact, the two Camerons were old friends, having known each other since 1991. As Cameron Pearson explained:

> **One of my friends dated her… and we spent a lot of double-dates together. When they stopped seeing each other, she and I kept in contact.**

Presumably helped by the Diaz factor, *Man Woman Film* did travel around the international film festival circuit from late January 1999 onwards, playing in Norway, the United States, Turkey, Portugal, Egypt, Argentina and Hungary. According to Pearson, the film attempted to combine French New Wave cinema with tragic farce. The vague story involves a young aspiring novelist, his pop star girlfriend, epilepsy, insanity, over-talkative mime artists and radical politics. The character names include 'Frustrated café poet', 'Kurtz: rapist of mannequins', 'Man in a dress', 'Anti-James Mason' and 'Gestapo mime and sex cult freak'. Heavy stuff.

Cast as 'Random Celebrity', Diaz appears in two short scenes, both shot in black and white. Reading poetry at a party, she is approached by one of the main characters. "You are very familiar," they say. "Of course," she replies, "I'm a celebrity." For her second scene, Diaz talks with a small boy, then meditates. *Man Woman Film* had a long, on-off shoot, and Diaz's hair style changes radically between her two appearances. All the other roles were played by students. Pearson claims, probably joking, that "They were deadly afraid of acting with Cameron D!" Running at just 83 minutes, *Man Woman Film* sounds like an intriguing prospect for the open-minded viewer.

Ever wanted to be someone else? More specifically, ever wanted to be a charismatic, bald American actor called John? This is the question posed by *Being John Malkovich* (1999), a strong contender for Cameron Diaz's weirdest movie to date. Both funny and disturbing, *Being John Malkovich* isn't the easiest film to enjoy, exploring some dark territory.

A co-production between Propaganda Films, Gramercy, Polygram and Single Cell Pictures, *Malkovich* marked the feature film debut of music video *auteur* Spike Jonze. Born Adam Spiegel, Jonze had worked with artists such as REM, Fatboy Slim and Bjork. The screenplay was by the little-known Charlie Kaufman, an experienced television writer, who also served as co-executive producer. *Malkovich* would be Kaufman's first movie script to reach the screen. The film was co-produced by REM frontman Michael Stipe, for whom Jonze had directed the 'Crush with Eyeliner' promo.

John Cusack starred as struggling street puppeteer-turned-filing clerk Craig Schwartz. Cusack's previous credits included *Grosse Pointe Blank* (1997), which he also co-wrote, *The Thin Red Line* (1998) and *Pushing Tin* (1999). Catherine Keener, who'd co-starred in *Out of Sight* (1998) and *8mm* (1999), took the part of Maxine Lund, Craig's duplicitous colleague and business partner. Looking for a change of pace, Cameron Diaz agreed to play the role of Lotte Schwartz, Craig's mousy, animal-fixated wife. For her, the part had a simple appeal: "I jumped at the chance to be unglamorous."

An animal lover herself – she has a pet cat called Little Man – Diaz nevertheless felt that Lotte had taken her pet obsession a little far. Interviewed by *Calgary Sun* reporter Louis B Hobson, she explained:

My character takes care of animals instead of herself. She is so concerned about her little charges that she forgets she has hair and has forgotten there's such a thing as make-up.

Cosmetics neglect aside, Diaz praised Charlie Kaufman's screenplay as a true original: "…it's been said that in Hollywood there are only 14 different scripts [that many?]. Well, this is number 15."

Of course, *Being John Malkovich* depended on the participation of the actual John Malkovich. Given that the actor had publicly dismissed film as a "shallow medium", this wasn't a foregone conclusion by any means. John Cusack had previously worked with Malkovich on the above-average action blockbuster *Con-Air* (1997). Cast as lead villain Cyrus 'The Virus' Grissom, Malkovich seemed comfortable enough with the shallowness around him. *Con-Air* is certainly preferable to the ill-fated Julia Roberts flop *Mary Reilly*, where Malkovich's mannered Dr Jekyll and Mr Hyde are difficult to tell apart. In any event, Malkovich liked Kaufman's script and agreed to take part. Budgeted at just $13 million, *Being John Malkovich* began shooting on 20 July 1998.

From the start, *Being John Malkovich* is an assured piece of filmmaking. The numerous puppet effects are impressive and there are amusing cameos from Charlie Sheen, Sean Penn and a briefly glimpsed Brad Pitt. Unable to make it as a professional puppeteer, Craig Schwartz is stuck among the filing cabinets of Lester Corp in Manhattan, New York. However, behind one dusty cabinet is a small door. Behind the door is a tunnel that leads directly into the head of John Malkovich. After quarter of an hour experiencing the world through Malkovich's eyes, Craig is unceremoniously deposited by the side of the New Jersey Turnpike.

While Craig ponders the metaphysical significance of his discovery, co-worker Maxine Lund suggests turning the Malkovich head experience into a lucrative after-hours business venture. Infatuated with Maxine, Craig agrees to the deal. $200 buys 15 minutes inside Malkovich's head. At first, the head trips prove a roaring success. When John Malkovich himself gives it a try, he finds himself in a restaurant full of Malkoviches, male and female. It's a mind-blower. Even Malkovich ends up stuck on the turnpike, where a passing truck driver lobs a beer can at his head, along with the advice: "Hey! Malkovich! Think fast!" Director Spike Jonze had intended to drop the scene from the film. Malkovich thought this throwaway moment was very funny, partly because it touched on his own childhood experience, and persuaded Jonze to keep it in the final cut. His favourite line in the movie is Maxine Lund's "Who the fuck is John Malkovich?" "I love that line."

Even before discovering the Malkovich portal, Craig Schwartz seems surrounded by general weirdness. He works on the cramped seventh-and-a-half floor of the strange Mertin

Above: *Lotte Schwartz – animal lover and would-be transsexual in Being John Malkovich.*

Building. His boss, Dr Lester (Orson Bean), announces that he is 105 years old and discusses his sexual fantasies in elaborate detail. Lester's receptionist claims not to understand what people say to her, though she seems sharp enough when Craig spurns her sexual advances: "Bastard." Adorned with long, lank hair, a stubbly beard and glasses, Craig Schwartz doesn't cut a dashing figure. Unfortunately, his character flaws amount to more than combining a jacket with jeans. Craig keeps puppets of himself, Lotte and Maxine in his workshop. As blatant symbolism goes, this is pretty direct. Craig is a megalomaniac control-freak-in-waiting. The Lotte puppet lies neglected in a dark corner, Craig busy playing with himself and Maxine. Craig's tenuous grasp of reality is established early on in the film. Not blessed with the soundest business sense, he fails to appreciate that puppet shows about sexual obsession won't draw the crucial family audience.

Peeking out from under one of the frumpiest wigs in film history, Diaz gives a fine performance as the kindly, awkward Lotte Schwartz. Spike Jonze goes all out to deglamorise Diaz. Aside from the wig, she is usually dressed in dowdy brown clothes. The scenes at the Schwartz apartment are staged in semi-gloom. An animal lover working in a pet shop, Lotte brings sick merchandise home with her, for round-the-clock nursing. Her current patients include a chimpanzee called Elijah and a parrot that mimics her: "Craig, honey, time to get up."

While Lotte is keen for Craig to find a steady job, she seems more concerned with boosting his self-esteem than bringing in extra money. Lotte talks wistfully of having a baby, only for Craig to mutter about the unfavourable economic climate. Her thwarted maternal instincts are channelled into animal care, centring on the nappy-clad Elijah the Chimp, who sometimes shares the Schwartzes' bed. A believer in animal psychiatry, Lotte has put Elijah into therapy. This is initially played for laughs, yet Elijah has a traumatic flashback to when he and his relatives were captured in the jungle.

Clad in her blue anorak, Lotte takes the second trip into John Malkovich, who's showering at the time. She gets turned on by the actor towelling himself down: "That's nice." Lotte is deeply affected by her Malkovich experience, finding a new sense of identity and assertiveness. For her, the Malkovich head portal is deeply sexual, in a feminine way: "he has a penis and a vagina…" Deciding that she's a frustrated transexual, Lotte will not be put off by Craig's objections: "Don't stand in the way of my actualisation as a man."

Lotte falls for Maxine via John Malkovich's head, competing with the lust-struck Craig for her affections. In fact Maxine is drawn to Lotte, but only as John

Malkovich. Likewise, she's attracted to Malkovich, providing Lotte's inside his head. This sort-of lesbian subplot leads to a bizarre three-way sexual encounter. Lotte moans with orgasmic ecstasy as she is dumped back at the New Jersey turnpike. As guest star Charlie Sheen puts it: "Hot lesbian witches. Think about it. It's fucking genius." Half-crazed with sexual jealousy, Craig eventually locks Lotte up inside Elijah's cage, while he seduces Maxine via Malkovich. Significantly, Maxine can't tell that she's being fooled.

Towards the end of *Being John Malkovich*, things are not looking good for the Lotte-Maxine romance. Unhappily married to Craig/Malkovich, a heavily pregnant Maxine keeps the Lotte puppet in her unborn child's cot. Hot for payback, a gun-wielding Lotte chases Maxine through Malkovich's subconscious. This takes in parental sex, high school locker room taunts, confinement in a cellar, an awful teenage date, pantie sniffing and pants-wetting on the school bus. It turns out that Maxine conceived when Lotte, not Craig, was inside Malkovich's head. This makes Lotte the baby's 'father', in a cerebral kind of way. There is a sort-of happy ending for Lotte, Maxine and their daughter. Things don't turn out so well for Craig. Tough.

Being John Malkovich received its world premiere at the Venice Film Festival on 2 September 1999. The film opened in the United States two months later, on 29 October. *Variety* critic David Rooney declared that *Malkovich* was "…so far out there it's almost off the scale". Boosted by some glowing reviews, the film grossed $23 million in the US, not a bad take for such an offbeat movie. Released in Britain on 17 March 2000, *Being John Malkovich* made £1.8 million. Even the *Sun*, not normally a patron of art-house fare, gave the film a rave review: "It's stupendous, fantastic… a work of insane genius."

The new millennium saw *Being John Malkovich* being showered with nominations for various awards. Spike Jonze, Charlie Kaufman and Catherine Keener were all nominated for Academy Awards. Kaufman subsequently won a BAFTA (British Academy of Film and Television Awards) for Best Original Screenplay. The leading cast members shared a Screen Actors Guild Award nomination for Outstanding Performance by a Cast in a Theatrical Motion Picture.

Diaz picked up a separate SAGA nomination for Outstanding Performance by a Female Actor in a Supporting Role. She also received an American Comedy Award nomination for Funniest Supporting Actress in a Motion Picture, an Online Film Critics Society Award nomination for Best Supporting Actress, and a Golden Satellite Award nomination for Best Performance by an Actress in a Supporting Role, Comedy or Musical. In addition, Diaz earned Golden Globe and BAFTA nominations, both for Best Performance by an Actress in a Supporting Role. Even the Las Vegas Film Critics Society handed her a Sierra Award nomination for Best Supporting Actress. Presumably, they didn't hold a grudge against Diaz for her brief participation in *Fear and Loathing in Las Vegas*.

While Diaz may have regretted the lack of actual wins, her status as a 'serious' film actor was now beyond doubt.

kickass angel

Now in demand for big-budget, high-profile movies, Cameron Diaz had no intention of abandoning the offbeat, independent school of filmmaking where she'd learned much of her craft. As she explained:

> I think that definitely your chances of coming across material in independent films – material that is more interesting and more challenging – is more likely than in big studio films. You always have to leave your doors open to independent films so you have that opportunity.

The success of *Being John Malkovich* fully endorsed this decision. On the downside, Diaz's ever-rising star status did not guarantee that she'd always get the parts she wanted. In late 1997, Diaz had auditioned for a co-starring role in *Waking the Dead* (2000), a character-based 1970s period piece. Based on a novel by Scott Spencer, the film tells the story of a devoted, politically committed couple, whose differing beliefs drive them apart, with tragic consequences. The director, Keith Gordon, had started out as an actor, getting his big break – sort of – in *Jaws 2* (1978). The flashback-heavy screenplay seemed to be celebrating the timelessness of love, which can transcend death itself.

Billy Crudup starred as Congressional candidate Fielding Pierce. As his closely fought campaign reaches its climax, Pierce starts having visions of his former lover, Sarah Williams, supposedly dead for nine years. Involved with the Chilean underground, she was killed in a car bomb explosion. Is she real, a ghost, a dream or a symptom of Pierce's guilt over selling out to the party system?

Cameron Diaz wanted the part of Sarah, an idealistic political activist who believes that change can only come from outside the system, which is inherently corrupt. Her violent, wasteful death opens the movie, Sarah's presence literally haunting subsequent events. To Diaz's disappointment, Keith Gordon cast Jennifer Connelly in the role. As with her previous rejections, Diaz took a philosophical view: "I think there's a lot of roles out there, and everybody gets what they're meant to get."

Waking the Dead took a long time to reach the screen. Though filming began in February 1998, the film didn't open in the US until 26 March 2000, over two years later. Given a limited release, *Waking the Dead* grossed only $327,400 in the States, disappearing from cinemas after three weeks. Diaz subsequently appeared in the similarly themed *Invisible Circus* (2001), which met with an equally muted response.

By contrast, Diaz had no problem turning down the female lead in Disney's *Inspector Gadget* (1999). This live-action version of the popular cartoon series starred Matthew Broderick as the humble security guard turned super Swiss-knife crime fighter. Diaz was offered the part of Dr. Brenda Bradford, a pioneering scientist who leads the government project behind the creation of Gadget. When she passed on the film, the role went to television actress Joely Fisher, who'd played a bit part in *The Mask*. Rupert Everett, Diaz's co-star from *My Best Friend's Wedding*, agreed to play the lead villain.

Diaz returned to the screen in Oliver Stone's epic American Football drama *Any*

Opposite: *Do you want some? Dylan (Drew Barrymore), Natalie (Cameron Diaz) and Alex (Lucy Liu), braced for action in Charlie's Angels.*

Left: With co-star Al Pacino in Any Given Sunday. "It was exciting and it was terrifying," said Diaz of the experience.

Given Sunday (1999). For this Warner release, she co-starred with Al Pacino, one of America's most charismatic and respected actors. Happy to take second billing, Diaz played Christina Pagniacci, owner of the fictional Miami Sharks. While Diaz never took up cheerleading, she did strut her stuff as a half-time dancer for high school football games. As the star explained to reporter Steve Tilley, she saw *Any Given Sunday* as a new departure for her acting career:

> It's dramatic, and that's what I've been sort of looking to get involved with, because I've done a lot of comedy and a lot of dark comedy and a lot of fantastical sort of ideas.

Oliver Stone hoped to make the film with the full co-operation of the National Football League (NFL). Wary of the director's controversial reputation, firmly cemented with the notorious *Natural Born Killers*

(1994), the image-conscious NFL refused to support the production. According to Stone, the NFL wouldn't allow him to use any of its football footage and pressured its sponsors to boycott the movie.

American Football movies have rarely been big box-office, especially outside the United States, where the game has never enjoyed wide popularity. For this reason, *Any Given Sunday* had to be made relatively cheaply. Working on a $62 million budget, Stone could not afford any big star salaries. Having signed on for the film prior to *There's Something About Mary*, Cameron Diaz cost the director a mere $500,000. Originally scheduled to begin shooting in May 1998, *Any Given Sunday* suffered a series of delays, finally going before the cameras in January 1999, eight months late. In the meantime, *There's Something About Mary* had hit the cinemas, turning Diaz into a fully fledged star. Both Al Pacino and Cameron Diaz stayed committed to *Any Given Sunday* throughout the setbacks. Impressed by Diaz's loyalty, Stone was also grateful that she didn't push for a pay rise to match her post-*Mary* star status.

Shooting on *Any Given Sunday* lasted a mere 65 days, a tight schedule for such an ambitious, large-scale production. According to Oliver Stone, Diaz felt extremely nervous prior to filming her first scene with Pacino. Diaz concurs:

That was crazy. I felt like a little girl, like a 12-year-old with braces while I was doing it. It was exciting and it was terrifying.

Well-known for speaking his mind, the director had nothing but praise for Diaz: "Cameron was great. She was a bonus to this film from beginning to end." Stone wanted her character to have both a cool business head and what he termed a "girlish anger". Always easygoing, with a good working attitude, Diaz gave exactly the performance Stone wanted. Other cast members were not quite so laid-back. During the filming of one football game, co-stars Jamie Foxx and L L Cool J got into a real fight, which made the national press. Diaz's only real problem with Stone was the director's tendency to reschedule scenes at the last minute. This led to two months of sitting around in Miami, just in case he needed her:

You never knew when you were going to be called in. You'd work four days and then have a week off and then work two days and have two weeks off.

Any Given Sunday displays Oliver Stone's trademark visceral, frenetic, in-your-face style. The director wanted his film to have a "vast, Promethean energy", and it certainly keeps moving. The driving soundtrack incorporates Native American chant, Metallica, Black Sabbath, Gary Glitter, Fatboy Slim and Modest Moussorgsky's 'Pictures at an Exhibition'. The movie veers into sensory overload, with over 3000 individual shots and 1000 digital effects. The football banter and tactics are not easy to follow for non-fans, which makes things even more confusing.

Like most of Stone's work, *Any Given Sunday* is at heart a buddy movie, filled with sentimental male bonding. Women don't get much of a look-in. Aside from Diaz's Christina, most of the female characters are players' wives or groupies, with the odd high-class hooker thrown in for good measure. Pacino plays veteran football coach Tony D'Amato, ageing, boozing, divorced and self-pitying. His beloved players, mostly black, are America's modern gladiators. While the death rate may be lower, there are some seriously nasty injuries, including a severed eyeball left on the astroturf. The crowd loves it. This isn't a game for wimps. According to D'Amato, football is the only real sanity: "Life is fucked". His life, maybe. American Football is a religious experience, a war zone and a metaphor for both American society and life in general. Running over two and a half hours, *Any Given Sunday* is never dull, which is an achievement of sorts.

Early on in *Any Given Sunday*, Christina Pagniacci is seen on the cover of *Forbes* magazine, along with the legend: 'Whatever It

ers who, in her view, can no longer cut it. For D'Amato, these are the men who helped build the team from nothing, and Christina's callous attitude outrages him. She doesn't respect the old ways, appreciate locker room etiquette or drink beer with the boys. Worse, Christina is personally disloyal to 'Uncle' D'Amato, whom she's known since childhood. According to Oliver Stone, D'Amato feels hurt that Christina has been changed – and corrupted – by the game's all-powerful "corporate structure". This is not a sentiment that would endear Stone to the NFL.

Christina inherited the Sharks from her father, a legendary team owner-manager killed by the stress of the game. Stone argues that this inheritance has proved as much a curse as a blessing for Christina. Lacking a son, the 'natural' heir to his team, Mr Pagniacci raised Christina like a boy: tough, competitive and a winner at any cost. Somewhere down the line, this conditioning messed with her head. The implication, of course, is that women and football management just don't mix. Diaz's own childhood experience of American football was entirely positive, watching games with her father. "He didn't have any sons; my sister and I kind of substituted for that."

Diaz more than holds her own against Pacino during their confrontational scenes together. Christina argues, with justification, that D'Amato is still living in the 1960s, when his career began. She also suggests that he resents her taking over a team he considers his own creation. While their methods differ, both feel they have the Sharks' best interests at heart. As Christina puts it: "I will do any-

Takes'. Proclaimed as 'Professional Football's Only Woman Owner', she is dressed in her trademark black, the team colour, against a blue backdrop, looking coolly determined. Christina certainly knows the game and her players, appearing brisk and efficient. She's also manipulative and ruthless. Feeling that the Miami Sharks have become a second-rate outfit, Christina wants to drop the older play-

Above: *Diaz power dresses for the* Any Given Sunday *premiere.*

thing… anything to bring this team back to greatness." She takes no shit from Miami's schmoozing mayor, threatening to relocate the Sharks to another city if he doesn't back her plans for a new stadium.

Any Given Sunday gave Diaz her first experience of on-screen nudity, though it was another actor who stripped off. During one locker room scene, Christina shakes hands with a stark naked player, whose major tackle is on full view, telling another: "Pete, don't stiffen up on me." Interviewed by *Winnipeg Sun* reporter Darryl Sterdan, Diaz made light of the experience:

All the women always ask about that scene. For some reason the men never do. That was one of those scenes where you just go in there and do your job – keep your eyes up, keep your spirits up.

She claimed not to have peeked during filming, only getting the full picture at the film's first screening. Diaz deserves full marks for going along with this scene, though it's too self-consciously casual about the full-frontal male nudity. As Diaz suggested: "I'm sure Oliver was trying to see how far he could take it. But I didn't have any problems. I can take it." Christina is subsequently propositioned by the Sharks' new star player, Willy Beamen (Jamie Foxx). As arrogant as he is talented, Beamen shows no sign of disappointment when Christina politely declines.

Oliver Stone has rarely provided decent parts for women and it's a tribute to Diaz that she makes something of a weakly conceived and written role. The script is so heavily slant-ed in the flawed-yet-noble D'Amato's favour that Christina becomes suspect in everything she does. While she is actively involved with the local inner city charities, it's hard to know if she's genuinely philanthropic or simply has an eye for good publicity. Stone wanted Christina to be "one tough customer", and she often comes across as a hard-hearted, ball-busting bitch. At one point, Christina pushes the Sharks' doctor to pass a player fit for an important game, despite possible head injuries. In the same scene, she demands that ageing star player 'Cap' (Dennis Quaid) be thrown off the team on medical grounds. Most unforgivable of all, Christina plans to sell off the team, destroying her late father's dream. As one character puts it, with damning matter-of-factness: "You don't love football anyway."

It's no accident that Diaz is harshly lit at times, presumably to underline her cold, unfeeling nature. When the Miami Sharks play the Dallas Knights, a crucial game, Christina dresses in red, the colour of the opposing team. What a traitor. Stone isn't subtle. Guest star Charlton Heston, playing a hard-nosed league official, drives the point home: "I honestly believe that woman would eat her young." Even on her own terms, Christina screws up, plotting an 'illegal' move to Los Angeles for the Sharks that could ruin her career.

For all her outward calm, Christina seems to be suffering from a severe case of internal conflict. She silently weeps as her boozing mother (Ann-Margret) tells D'Amato that the game has cost her both her husband and her daughter, describing the adult Christina as "a tragedy". Even audiences unimpressed by D'Amato's old-style code of honour should be moved by this sad maternal condemnation. Despite Diaz's best efforts, this scene doesn't have the intended impact, with Stone unable to give it any sense of true emotion.

Christina doesn't appear to have much of a personal life away from the game, though Stone wrote the character as a married woman. In the finished film, there's a brief appearance from a male character who could be either her husband or lover. Stone felt that it wasn't important to spell this out. The director also wanted to imply that Christina has lesbian tendencies, the second time in the space of two films for Diaz. Once again, this isn't evident in the final cut.

Just as Willy Beamen learns the true meaning of team spirit, the D'Amato way, Christina rediscovers her principles and humanity, clutching a symbolic cute white dog. As the closing credits roll, Christina renounces her bad ways at a press conference:

"I want to live up to what it is my father left me." She even publicly thanks D'Amato for "helping me understand again what I had forgotten". Stone claims that Christina will genuinely miss Uncle Tony, who's leaving the Miami Sharks to coach a team in New Mexico. It's all so heartwarming.

Any Given Sunday's promotion matched the movie for subtlety and understatement: 'Life Is A Contact Sport. Play. Or Be Played.' Released in the United States on 26 December 1999, the film didn't make it to British cinemas until 2 April 2000. The domestic gross of $75.53 million disappoint-ed Stone, who felt the movie could have made over $100 million in the States with better timing. In Britain, *Any Given Sunday* met with mixed reviews and indifferent box-office. *Time Out* critic Nick Bradshaw dis-missed the film as "a meathead burlesque". On the positive side, Diaz subsequently won the 2000 ALMA Award for Outstanding Actress in a Feature Film, and the 2000 Blockbuster Entertainment Award for Favorite Actress – Drama.

Shortly before *Any Given Sunday* opened in the United States, Diaz experienced a little off-screen drama. In December 1999, she ran into trouble at Los Angeles International Airport, when her passport and a large amount of cash were stolen. Fortunately, police soon tracked down the culprit, an air-line security guard. This inconvenient, yet minor, episode received only token press cov-erage. To the disappointment of tabloid jour-nalists everywhere, Diaz's personal life has been low on scandal. At the age of 17, she became involved with video producer Carlos de La Torre and stayed with him for five years. Her more high-profile romance with Matt Dillon seemed an ideal match, if their public comments were to be believed. Interviewed by Bruce Kirkland while promoting *There's Something About Mary*, Dillon sang Diaz's praises to an almost embarrassing degree:

She's idealised but she's not like the Hitchcock ice goddess... She's warm. She's beautiful and she's sexy... She has a good sense of humour. She's very feminine. She's really well balanced and I think that's why she's an ideal girl.

Diaz fully repaid the compliment, explaining that Dillon's long experience in the film industry helped her greatly: "Matt is incredible for me to be with at this moment in my life… He knows what kind of demands the business puts on a person."

While the relationship lasted nearly three years, there were persistent rumours of Dillon's alleged infidelity. One report had him getting intimate with troubled pop diva Mariah Carey in a New York nightclub, hardly the most private arena. Hard-rock fan Diaz once commented: "If you really want to torture me, sit me in a room, strapped to a chair, and put Mariah Carey on." Presumably, Matt Dillon felt differently.

It probably didn't help that Diaz was based in Los Angeles while Dillon remained in Manhattan, 3000 miles away. At the time, Diaz claimed that the arrangement suited her well: "I've been living out of a suitcase for too many years. I wanted my own home desperately and now I have two." Both attempted to commute over the vast distance, yet this coast-to-coast arrangement eventually became unworkable. After a short engagement, Diaz and Dillon went their separate ways. Diaz stayed tight-lipped about the reasons for the break-up, which only increased the press speculation.

In early 1999, following a short fling with *Any Given Sunday* director Oliver Stone, Diaz began dating fellow actor Jared Leto. During breaks in the *Sunday* shoot, she would fly from Miami to Toronto, where Leto was filming *American Psycho* (2000). Not yet a big name in Hollywood, Leto has appeared in *The Thin Red Line* (1998), *Girl, Interrupted* (1999) and *Requiem for a Dream* (2000). He is probably best known for his supporting role as 'Angel Face' in *Fight Club* (1999), where he is beaten to a bloody pulp by Edward Norton. Strangely enough, Norton and Diaz had briefly been an item. Leto's more harmonious offscreen relationship with Diaz blossomed, as she explained to the media:

Jared's terrific. We have a great time going out, dancing, doing things I really like. With Jared I don't have to worry about his moods.

Which suggests that former lovers such as Matt Dillon were less easy to handle. The happy couple became engaged in November 2000. This seemed to scotch rumours that Diaz had nearly split with Leto over his extreme preparations for *Requiem for a Dream*. Cast as a hardcore drug addict, Leto supposedly insisted on giving up sex while working on the film. In July 2001, the American tabloid press published allegations that Leto had cheated on Diaz. These were quickly dismissed by Diaz, who insisted that the relationship was as strong as ever:

We're very happy. We've been together two and a half years. These stories hurt Jared more than they hurt me. I'm used to it.

Whatever the truth of this, Diaz and Leto parted company shortly afterwards. According to the press stories, Leto had been caught with another woman at the Paris Hilton. Or possibly with a woman called Paris Hilton. So much for accurate reporting.

Left: *Carol and her police detective sister Kathy (Amy Brenneman) in* Things You Can Tell Just by Looking at Her.

Being the 'ideal' woman has proved as much a curse as a blessing for Diaz's love life.

Following the brash, testosterone-heavy *Any Given Sunday*, Diaz appeared in the much more low-key *Things You Can Tell Just by Looking at Her* (2000). The film was written and directed by former cameraman Rodrigo Garcia, who'd developed the project with a grant from Robert Redford's Sundance Institute. Industry major MGM/UA liked the finished script enough to finance the production. Shot on location in and around Los Angeles, *Things You Can Tell…* consists of five episodes, centring on a disparate group of women living in the San Fernando Valley. We have a doctor, a bank manager, a police detective, a single mother and a lesbian tarot card reader. The big-name cast included Glenn Close, *Ally McBeal* star Calista Flockhart and Holly Hunter, who'd worked with Diaz on *A*

Life Less Ordinary.

Diaz appears in the final story, 'Love Waits for Kathy', as Carol, the blind sister of Kathy (Amy Brenneman), a lonely police detective. Kathy investigates the suicide of an old school friend, who seems to have killed herself out of loneliness. Carol, a shrewd judge of human nature, also tries to work out the reason.

Even critics who disliked the overall film singled out Diaz for praise. She gives a zesty performance as Carol, a positive, life-affirming young woman who will not be constrained by her disability. An accomplished piano player and teacher, Carol is determined to have a similarly successful personal life. Stood up by one date, Carol is not deterred. The able-bodied Kathy, by contrast, is afraid to risk exposing her feelings. The movie overdoes the heavy irony and blatant symbolism at times, the sightless Carol able to 'see' things

Right: Diaz as blind music teacher Carol in Things You Can Tell Just by Looking at Her.

that her highly trained policewoman sister cannot. Running a brisk 80 minutes, *Things You Can Tell...* is kept afloat by generally strong performances and an underplayed humour that balances the serious tone.

The film received its world premiere at the Sundance Film Festival on 22 January 2000. Largely well reviewed, it also attracted favourable attention at the Cannes Film Festival. Uncertain about the movie's commercial potential, MGM/UA decided not to give it a theatrical release, arguing that it stood little chance against the summer blockbusters. Instead, the studio sold the film straight to the Showtime cable television channel, ensuring a little public exposure before it hit video and DVD. At least the publicity department came up with a provocative tagline: 'A Man Only Sees What a Woman Wants Him to Know.'

Once upon a time there was a 1970s television series about three female private investigators and their mysterious millionaire boss. The stars were Farrah Fawcett, Kate Jackson and Jaclyn Smith. The show wasn't that great but the mix of glamour, action and jokes proved a winner. Twenty years later, the idea was revived for the movies, bigger and bolder than ever before. *Charlie's Angels* (2000) took a stale format and brought it back to ass-kicking life. Offering high velocity stunts, gravity-defying kung fu fighting, state-of-the-art digital effects, a poptastic soundtrack and a strong dose of humour, the movie goes places undreamed of by the original series. Playing one of the least likely undercover agents in movie history, top Angel Cameron Diaz takes time out from the crime-busting to dance in her Spiderman underwear. Life doesn't get much better.

Charlie's Angels was one of those Hollywood projects that hung around for a long time before getting a studio green-light. It probably didn't help that the TV-show-to-blockbuster-film genre had a very mixed box-office track record. For every smash hit like *Mission: Impossible* (1996) there was a less impressive *Lost in Space* (1998) or even outright flops like *The Avengers* (1998). At one time, Demi Moore intended to lead a new band of Angels on the big screen, before her declining star status ruled her out. Eventually, former child actor Drew Barrymore took over the project, as both producer and star, and made a deal with Columbia Tristar through her own Flower Films company. Budgeted at a cool $92 million, *Charlie's Angels* The Movie had to be a blockbuster just to recover its production cost.

While Barrymore had no problem persuading Diaz to come on board, casting the third Angel proved a long and difficult task. A number of proposed co-stars came and went, notably Catherine Zeta-Jones, Halle Berry, Angelina Jolie, Liv Tyler, Jada Pinkett, Lauryn Hill and Thandie Newton. Even the easygoing Diaz eventually showed signs of impatience: "…somebody's got to make a decision real soon." The new Angels line-up was finally completed by Lucy Liu, from the hit television show *Ally McBeal*. Diaz signed on for a hefty $12 million fee and the chance to relive some childhood fantasies. As she explained:

I was at kindergarten when it was first out. My sister would play Farrah because she had long hair. I would play whatever my sister would let me play. Usually Bosley.

This time around, the role of Bosley, Charlie's ever-loyal frontman, went to veteran comedy actor Bill Murray. The supporting cast included *Friends* star Matt LeBlanc, playing Lucy Liu's conceited actor boyfriend.

Looking for a director, Barrymore settled on Joseph McGinty Nichol, better known as McG. Specialising in music videos, McG had worked with Korn, Barenaked Ladies, The Offspring, Smash Mouth and Sugar Ray. *Charlie's Angels* would be his feature film debut. Looking to achieve the same kind of high-gear 'party' style for the movie, McG displayed non-stop enthusiasm and energy during production, applauding after virtually every shot.

For the high energy fight scenes, the stars underwent three months of intensive training – eight hours a day, six days a week – under the instruction of Chinese martial arts master Yuen Cheung Yan. McG took much of his inspiration for the kung fu-style action from the Hong Kong movie *Iron Monkey* (1993). This martial arts classic was directed by Cheung Yan's brother, Yuen Woo Ping, who'd recently fight-choreographed both *The Matrix* (1999) and *Crouching Tiger, Hidden Dragon* (2000). As well as learning basic martial arts moves, the trainee Angels had to master wire-harness flying, which would give the impression of super-human agility on screen. This fast-track course in screen super-fighting came at a price. From the outset, Diaz knew that she, Barrymore and Liu were in for a tough time:

Our trainer said, 'We're going to introduce you to your new best friend. You will learn to love him, embrace him,

'and know him by name.' We asked, 'Who is it?' 'Pain' was the reply.

A natural athlete, Diaz was very quick to pick up the intricate fight choreography. British stunt co-ordinator Vic Armstrong praised Diaz for the elegance of her moves. By the time shooting began in January 2000, all three stars could handle the comic-book kung fu, though several of Barrymore's high kicks plainly miss their intended target.

During production, Diaz discovered that being an action heroine had a major effect on her wardrobe choices:

> There were times when I'd go, 'This outfit would look so badass with stilettos.' You wanted those four-inch heels, those wrappy, strappy, show-off-your-pedicure shoes, but you couldn't do it. At the beginning of the scene it would have been fine because I'm just hanging out with the dude. But the next thing you know, you're kicking the dude's rear, so you had to make sure you had the right shoes on.

Like many big movie productions, *Charlie's Angels* was dogged by stories of star tantrums, behind-the-scenes strife and in-fighting. Rumours surfaced that Bill Murray had walked off the film after a violent row with Lucy Liu. There seems to have been some basis in fact for this much-exaggerated tabloid filler story. Shooting the first scene at the Charles Townsend Agency without a finished script, the cast and crew weren't sure how the sequence should play. According to director

Above: *Lucy Liu, Drew Barrymore and Diaz arrive at the* Charlie's Angels *premiere.*

McG, Murray and Liu had a very "intense" discussion about the character interplay. For the record, the finished film shows little sign of production problems, though Bosley is notably absent from several key agency scenes, where his character would logically be present. That said, logic isn't really what *Charlie's Angels* is about.

The trailer for *Charlie's Angels* advised audiences to 'Get Some Action!' The movie itself is top-flight escapist fantasy, with the

emphasis on non-stop entertainment. Rejoicing in its own frivolity, *Charlie's Angels* is the best kind of tongue-in-cheek kitsch, where the crime-busting leads never look likely to smear their lip gloss, let alone lose their lives. While hardly the greatest female role models, the new look Angels easily outclass most of the men they encounter, flashing a little cleavage now and then in the line of duty. Co-star Bill Murray describes the film as "girls having fun", which is pretty accurate.

Setting *Charlie's Angels* in a hyper-reality 'Angel World', McG wanted a cartoonish, storybook visual quality with bright colour schemes. The style is part James Bond, part Austin Powers and several parts *The Matrix*, especially when the fists and feet start to fly. Displaying a sense of 'cool' absent from the TV show, the movie has enough confidence in itself to poke fun at the whole TV-to-film genre. Faced with *T.J. Hooker: The Movie* as the in-flight entertainment, one disgruntled airline passenger remarks: "Another movie from an *old* TV show", then jumps out of the plane.

Nods to the television series include the Angels' trademark slow-motion hair-tossing and the casting of John Forsythe, the original voice of the unseen Charlie. The props department even located the phone speaker box from the television show, through which Charlie always addressed the Angels. Farrah Fawcett, Kate Jackson and Jaclyn Smith all turned down the chance to make cameo appearances. Probably for the best. If it matters, the deliberately preposterous storyline involves stolen voice-ID software and a plot to murder Charlie.

Generally well reviewed, *Charlie's Angels*

attracted its share of critical sniping. Some felt that Murray was disappointing as Bosley, his subdued performance and on-off participation in the action reflecting the supposed on-set clashes. On the other hand, Crispin Glover's spooky Thin Man, who never utters a word, is a quality villain. Having survived several clashes with the Angels, not to mention a race-car plunge off a tall bridge, the Thin Man is finally blown up by his own boss. Who says crime pays? Short on meaningful statements, *Charlie's Angels* may be mindless fun but it's good mindless fun.

In terms of character appeal, *Charlie's Angel's* biggest asset is undoubtedly Cameron Diaz, who more than earns her top-billing. The wholesome, good-natured, borderline kooky Natalie Cook makes an effective contrast to the street-smart Dylan Sanders (Drew Barrymore) and the upper-class Alex Munday (Lucy Liu). Towering above her fellow kick-ass Angels, Natalie is a sunny, fresh-faced California girl, who also happens to be a linguist, ornithologist and top-grade secret agent. Faced with a particularly hazardous assignment, one client is sceptical: "Sounds impossible." Natalie has no such reservations: "Sounds like fun."

First seen piloting a vast motorboat in a skimpy bikini, Natalie gets to adopt various high-fashion disguises: geisha, cocktail waitress, racing driver, belly dancer, rock chick drummer, Swiss Miss yodel-a-gram and male business executive. A real-life racing car enthusiast, Diaz certainly looks at home behind the wheel. Her hair colour changes along with the outfits, though the hair fetishist Thin Man has no problem recognis-

Above: Lucy Liu, Cameron Diaz and Drew Barrymore in Charlie's Angels. *"You had to make sure you had the right shoes on," says Diaz.*

ing Natalie on the race track. She also demonstrates the figure-enhancing properties of a white lycra bodysuit and a black wetsuit.

Natalie isn't given much in the way of background, though the opening credits sequence shows her in dental braces, terrifying a driving instructor with a nifty piece of two-wheel car-balancing. What the film does reveal is that even secret agents have their fantasies. Natalie dreams of being a disco diva, dancing to the sound of 'Heaven Must Be Missing an Angel'. In Angel World, dreams come true, and Natalie's unorthodox dance style soon has the normally impassive Soul Train crowd chanting "Go white girl!"

Unlike Dylan and Alex, Natalie retains a wide-eyed innocence in the face of the script's barrage of sexual innuendo, telling one hunky mailman: "You can just feel free to stick things in my slot." Diaz's expert delivery of this throwaway dirty joke earned her a 2001 MTV Movie Award nomination for Best Line from a Movie. Natalie is also the only Angel to have something resembling a normal relationship, teaming up with Pete (Luke Wilson), a down-to-earth barman and all-round nice guy. If nothing else, *Charlie's Angels* demonstrates the difficulties of balancing a top secret crime-fighting career and a personal life, Natalie taking a call from Pete on her mobile phone while busting Bosley from a jail cell.

Interestingly, Diaz disliked her dialogue during Natalie's epic hand-to-hand fight with the villainous Vivian Wood (Kelly Lynch), who poses as a client in order to track down Charlie. Still on the phone to Pete, Natalie is enraged when Vivian casually smashes her mobile: "Do you know how hard it is to find a quality man in Los Angeles?" McG agreed to drop the line if preview audiences didn't laugh, only to find that it played well at test screenings. It certainly adds a little more spice to a film that, in the director's words, "explodes the pleasure centre of the audience's brain".

Charlie's Angels opened in the United States on 5 November 2000, taking an impressive $40 million over its first weekend. Obliged to wait another three weeks, British audiences proved equally enthusiastic. The film grossed $125 million in the US and an additional $100 million overseas, around $18 million of which came from the UK.

Cameron Diaz and Lucy Liu later attended Drew Barrymore's wedding to comedian-actor Tom Green. The happy couple had met while filming *Charlie's Angels*, in which Green played the small role of Chad, Dylan Sanders' spaced-out boyfriend. While Barrymore and Green got it together on-screen, their real-life union proved short-lived.

Back in Angel World, the success story continued. In 2001, the Academy of Science Fiction, Fantasy & Horror Films gave Diaz a Saturn Award nomination for Best Supporting Actress. Why not Best Actress? She also received a third Golden Satellite Award nomination, for Best Performance by an Actress in a Motion Picture, Comedy or Musical. All three *Charlie's Angels* stars shared a Blockbuster Entertainment Award for Favorite Action Team, and an MTV Movie Award for Best On-Screen Team. On her own, Diaz won the MTV Movie Award for Best Dance Sequence. Go white girl.

The success of *Charlie's Angels* inevitably prompted calls for a sequel, involving as many of the original cast and crew as possible. Most crucially, Columbia wanted to reunite the hit *Angels* line-up of Drew Barrymore, Cameron Diaz and Lucy Liu. While the 1970s television series had survived three major cast changes, the original trio remained the most popular. In November 2001, it was reported that McG had agreed to direct the follow-up, while Diaz was committed "in principle" to reprising her character. Columbia hoped to release *Charlie's Angels 2* in either late 2002 or early 2003. A month later, *Daily Variety* announced that Diaz had signed on for the sequel, picking up a cool $20 million pay cheque. Producer and co-star Drew Barrymore was already on board, while third Angel Lucy Liu remained "in talks", presumably to boost her salary. Whether or not Liu returned, shooting on *Angels 2* would begin in summer 2002. Now rivalling former co-star Julia Roberts as the world's highest paid actress, Cameron Diaz had good reason to shake her Angel booty one more time.

Opposite: The Charlie Angels stars pick up their Favourite Action Team trophies at the 2001 Blockbuster Entertainment Awards.

beautiful ugly

Cameron Diaz isn't really the star of *The Invisible Circus* (2001), though she's certainly the dominant presence. Based on a novel by Jennifer Egan, this low-key Fine Line release is a depressing tale of 1960s idealism and 1970s disillusion. The title refers to what one character describes as an "adult funhouse" of soft drugs, trippy music and performance art. The Invisible Circus was a real sixties 'happening', staged in a deconsecrated church in downtown San Francisco. Writer-director Adam Brooks, a big fan of the book, intended his film to blend elements of the road movie, period drama, offbeat romance and radical politics.

Invisible Circus is so obviously a labour of love that criticism seems almost unfair. Despite some touching moments, however, the film has little new to say about family relationships, the death of the sixties dream or the search for identity. Shot more than six months before *Charlie's Angels*, *Invisible Circus* sat on the shelf for some time, and it's not hard to see why.

Adorned with a long brown wig, Diaz plays Faith, who leaves the 1969 San Francisco hippie scene for a tour of Europe and a journey of self-discovery. Months later, her body is found on the rocks below a small Portuguese fishing village. No one knows if Faith's tragic death was an accident, suicide or even murder. Seven years later, her younger sister, Phoebe (Jordana Brewster), decides to find out, enlisting the reluctant assistance of Faith's former boyfriend, 'Wolf' (Christopher Eccleston).

Despite the downbeat tone, New Line Cinema liked the storyline of *Invisible Circus*, making a deal with Adam Brooks in early 1998. The company's long association with

Cameron Diaz probably helped with her casting. In the event, Diaz loved Brooks' script, which she found extremely moving: "At the end of it… I cried. It touched me so many times throughout." The closeness of the two sisters at the heart of the story echoed her own relationship with Chimene. Praising the characters as "beautifully written", she also admired the unusual flashback structure. Brooks felt that the part of Faith was a good dramatic role for Diaz, whom he described as a "free spirit". As the director explained: "Faith just has star quality and you need someone in that part who gives that off without working at it."

Adam Brooks' previous screenwriting credits included *Practical Magic* (1998), with Nicole Kidman and Sandra Bulloch, and *Beloved* (1998), starring Oprah Winfrey and Thandie Newton, who later made the *Charlie's Angels* short-list. Like *Invisible Circus*, these films feature women in dominant, if troubled roles, though *Practical Magic* is weak on substance.

Invisible Circus also gave Diaz a chance to revisit Paris, where she'd lived briefly during her world tour in the late 1980s. Along with many of the cast and crew, she did extensive research into the 1960s, a decade Diaz missed by three years, looking at documentaries, books and interviews. By the end, Diaz understood the idealism that had driven Faith's generation: "…we are making a difference, we are going forward, we are… doing something that's never been done before". Brooks saw Diaz as the perfect embodiment of this spirit: "She's very special and she shines." The film began shooting in May 1999, production lasting nine weeks.

Opposite: With co-star Christina Applegate in The Sweetest Thing.

The title sequence of *Invisible Circus* has an effective dreamlike quality, the barefoot Faith dancing in slow motion against a blue sky. Stuck at home watching *The Rockford Files*, Phoebe wants to come to terms with the loss of Faith and find her own identity. As Jordana Brewster explained during filming: "She still has that [idealised] image of her sister, put up on a pedestal." Before leaving San Francisco, Phoebe sleeps in her dead sister's bedroom, still exactly as Faith left it. Phoebe retraces Faith's route through Europe, looking for information on her in Paris and Amsterdam.

Off screen for much of the film, Cameron Diaz contributes a regular voice-over, Faith reading out the postcards she sent to Phoebe years earlier as the latter looks at the same places. Living in San Francisco, hippie capital of the world, Faith embraced the counter-culture and its spirit of peaceful revolution, marching for the Civil Rights Movement and protesting against the Vietnam War. Likeable, compassionate and idealistic, she later became dangerously naïve.

Interviewed during production on *Invisible Circus*, Diaz argued that Faith is too full of life and energy ever to be content, always wanting something more. Feeling that soft drugs and endless parties were not enough, Faith wanted to be a 'true' anarchist. Now living in West Berlin, she got involved with the Red Army, a radical political group that robbed banks and listened to reggae music. In one of the film's more unlikely scenes, Faith attempts to cut through a wire fence while dressed in 'square' clothes and a blonde wig.

There are too many unresolved subplots and subtexts in *Invisible Circus* for the story to

really click. Phoebe envied Faith's bond with their late father, a frustrated artist who toiled in a dull corporate job before succumbing to leukaemia at an early age. Feeling that he'd wasted his life, Faith's dad advised her to follow her passions without hesitation, leading to her own premature death. Just as Faith pursued her father's dream, so Phoebe is now chasing her sister's ghost. During her Amsterdam visit, Phoebe hallucinates Faith's smiling, beckoning figure while tripping on a free sample of LSD. She later makes advances to Wolf, as if she were recreating and possibly improving Faith's life. After token resistance, he gives in.

There is a bleak contrast between the optimism and rebellion of the late 1960s and the disappointment, confusion and conformity of the 1970s. Wolf, who put away his Union Jack coat and cut his hair a long time ago, has settled in Paris. He has a job, an apartment and a Faith lookalike girlfriend. Wolf doesn't seem truly content, yet has learned to accept life's inevitable compromises.

For all its good intentions, *Invisible Circus* is undermined by a flimsy screenplay and some serious miscasting. While Diaz holds her scenes together, sounding believably fluent in German, Jordana Brewster lacks the experience and presence to carry the rest of the movie. A newcomer to feature films, having made her debut in the enjoyable science fiction thriller *The Faculty* (1998), Brewster needed more guidance than director Brooks provided. The script doesn't develop her character, Phoebe simply reacting to past events. Sharing little screen-time, Diaz and Brewster don't look like sisters and the movie fails to make their relationship ring true.

Right: Recording her character voice for Shrek.

The final third of *Invisible Circus* drags badly, building up to a 'shock' revelation that seems a distinct let-down. Declaring her late father to be a 'murder' victim of the capitalist system, Faith became increasingly impulsive, selfish and reckless. Involved with another West German anarchist group, she agreed to plant a bomb in the offices of an arms dealer (both effective and ironic). Believing the building to be empty, she later discovered that a young accountant was killed in the explosion. Unable to deal with her guilt at taking a life, Faith 'sacrificed' herself to atone for her crime. Perhaps some mysteries are best left unexplained.

The Invisible Circus premiered at the Sundance Film Festival on 26 January 2001. This crucial first screening had been delayed, allegedly because of editing problems during post-production. A week later, the film went on limited release in New York and Los Angeles. The trailer was misleadingly action-packed, turning off audiences who might appreciate the movie and disappointing anyone expecting to see Cameron Diaz in fighting mode. In the event, the film grossed only $55,388 during the first weekend of its US release and went straight to DVD and video in Britain.

While *Invisible Circus* passed most audiences by, just about everyone with access to a cinema, VCR or DVD player has seen *Shrek* (2001), a *bona fide* computer-animation classic. For the first time since *The Mask*, Cameron Diaz played opposite a green-faced monster with a sentimental streak. *Shrek* is loosely based on a short illustrated book by William Steig, first published in 1990. The story involves a gruff, yet good-natured green ogre, his motor-mouthed donkey sidekick and a spirited captive princess who is not all she seems. If this sounds like a traditional fairy-tale premise, the end result is something else. Any film that pokes fun at both Walt Disney and blaxploitation movies in the space of one joke has to be good. Incidentally, 'Shrek' is Yiddish for 'monster'.

Shrek was produced by PDI-Dreamworks, which had previously made the hit computer-animation feature *Antz* (1998). *Austin Powers* star Mike Myers led the impressive voice cast, giving Shrek a distinct Scottish accent. The part was originally intended for comedian Chris Farley, who, like Myers, first came to prominence on the popular television show *Saturday Night Live*. In need of a breakthrough movie hit, Farley signed on for *Shrek* and recorded his dialogue. But the seriously overweight comic had become increasingly dependent on drugs and died shortly afterwards. Under the circumstances, Dreamworks felt it best to recast the part.

The role of Donkey went to Eddie Murphy, another ex-*Saturday Night Live* player, who'd recently revived his flagging movie career with two comedy remakes, *The Nutty Professor* (1996) and *Dr Dolittle* (1998). Cast as Princess Fiona, Cameron Diaz took third place in the star billing, below Myers and Murphy. Cartoon voice-over work does not pay big bucks by Hollywood standards, as Robin Williams discovered when he provided the voice of the Genie for Disney's *Aladdin* (1992). Diaz received a $1.5 million fee for *Shrek*, plus a percentage of the box-office gross.

Budgeted at $60 million, *Shrek* took three years to make, employing around 300 artists and technicians. The producers wanted live-action-style camerawork and a high level of picture detail and texture. The original character design for Princess Fiona was much more stylised than the final version, with huge 'anime' eyes and a tiny waist. The directors abandoned this approach in favour of a more or less naturalistic figure. One of the biggest challenges was to get Fiona's emerald green dress and red-brown hair to move in a believable fashion. Perfecting the design and movement of the Princess took a full year. Diaz gave the end result her full approval: "I

thought 'wow', that's just so realistic." She particularly liked the way that Fiona had the same mannerisms and bearing as herself.

The character voices were recorded over 18 months. Schedule clashes meant that the lead actors had to record their lines separately. This isn't evident in the finished film, where Shrek, Donkey and Fiona have a strong interplay. Given that the animated characters were already caricatures, the directors felt the actors should use their normal voices, rather than attempt 'cartoonish' accents. Having recorded his dialogue with this in mind, Mike Myers later suggested redubbing his lines in a Scottish accent, which he felt would suit Shrek better. After a few trial takes, the filmmakers agreed, though this last-minute change supposedly cost the production an extra $4 million. The voice isn't a million miles away from the one Myers used as 'Fat Bastard' in *Austin Powers – The Spy Who Shagged Me* (1999). Myers improvised much of his dialogue, lending Shrek's conversation a spontaneous quality.

Producer Aron Warner described Cameron Diaz as "really fun to work with". Co-director Andrew Adamson felt she was "a wonderful, down-to-earth... very real person". Adamson drew comparisons between Diaz and Princess Fiona, both star and character retaining their values and humanity in seductive, unreal, often treacherous worlds. During one recording session, Diaz asked a crew member to pull on her arm for the scene where Shrek drags Fiona through a dragon's castle. Something of a perfectionist, Diaz wanted the physical sensation to make her vocal performance as believable as possible.

Shrek opens with a fairy-tale picture

book, telling a familiar story: "Once upon a time there was a lovely princess." This particular princess is imprisoned by a dragon, in a castle surrounded by lava. Tearing out a page of the book to use as toilet paper, Shrek isn't convinced, emerging from the lavatory as the main credits roll. The contemporary rock score and hip, knowing in-jokes suggest this movie isn't going to be a typical fairy story. *Shrek* is set in the mythical land of Duloc, where fairy-tale characters are being persecuted by the evil human ruler, Lord Farquaad (John Lithgow). Pinocchio, the Three Blind Mice, the Three Bears, the Three Little Pigs, Snow White and the Seven Dwarfs and even the Big Bad Wolf are all fugitives from the short-arsed tyrant. In one scene, Farquaad tortures an innocent gingerbread man for information, dipping him in milk. Mama Bear ends up as a rug on Farquaad's bedroom floor.

The character design in *Shrek* is impressive. Shrek, Donkey and Fiona all have very expressive faces. The human characters are much more realistic than the computer-generated people seen in the groundbreaking *Toy Story* (1995). The fiercely independent Princess Fiona doesn't look much like Cameron Diaz, her red-brown hair underlining their physical differences. According to the Magic Mirror dating service, Princess Fiona is partial to pina coladas. She also lets out the odd belch. Diaz did her own burping for the movie, winning a 2001 Nickelodeon Award for Best Belch. This top-grade burp wasn't recorded specially for the scene, Diaz delivering an unscripted belch during one recording session.

Fiona certainly isn't the typical damsel in distress. At one point, she sings to a bluebird

Above: *Arriving at the premiere of Shrek, in April 2001.*

so shrilly that the poor creature explodes. Initially taken aback, the ever-practical Princess fries up the bird's unhatched eggs and serves them for breakfast. Confronted with a high-camp Robin Hood (Vincent Cassel) and his equally flamboyant band of Merry Men, Fiona takes them out with a fine display of gravity-defying, time-freezing martial arts. This looks like a homage to Diaz's role in *Charlie's Angels* but wasn't meant as such. *Shrek*'s makers had intended to base the fight scene on Jackie Chan movies. The veteran Hong Kong action star was now a hot Hollywood property after the success of *Rumble in the Bronx* (1995) and *Rush Hour* (1998). During *Shrek*'s lengthy production, however, both *The Matrix* and *Crouching Tiger, Hidden Dragon* hit the screens, providing further inspiration. Having taught the Sherwood Forest Irregulars a hard lesson, Fiona has to remove an arrow from Shrek's gigantic butt, which isn't so cool.

For all her own cliché-busting, Fiona is disappointed that Shrek doesn't stick to the fairy-tale rules. The ogre offers no hint of romance, let alone the "true love's kiss" she's been waiting for. Fiona's diehard faith in tradition makes her seem naïve, pushy and downright ungrateful at times. As Fiona and Shrek grow closer, she presents him with a spider's web candy floss, liberally decorated with juicy flies. In return, Shrek blows up a snake into a living balloon for her to fly. The snake looks okay about the whole thing. They even eat roasted weed rat together, the tails dangling from their lips (now that's attention to detail).

Fairy tales require a little heartbreak and the Princess hides a secret she considers shameful. Under a powerful enchantment, Fiona turns into an ogre at night. Believing that marriage to a handsome king – or even Lord Farquaad – will lift the curse, Fiona can't see that she's already met her true love. After a series of misunderstandings and a sober meditation on the nature of true beauty, *Shrek* gets into high gear for the finale. There can't be many royal weddings where a huge dragon smashes its head through a stained glass window and eats the groom. Farquaad had it coming. It's to *Shrek*'s credit that the ending doesn't cop out. While Disney would probably turn both Shrek and Fiona into 'beautiful people', this movie leaves them both as ogres, beautiful to each other. As the closing caption puts it: "And they lived ugly ever after." Having made her film debut opposite a green-faced 'monster', Cameron Diaz finally got to play one.

Released in the United States on 20 May 2001, *Shrek* grossed a hefty $40.3 million during its opening weekend. Taking over $267 million at the North American box-office, the film subsequently doubled its gross with video and DVD rentals and sales. Hitting British cinema screens on 1 July 2001, *Shrek* earned nearly £30 million from its UK theatrical run. In February 2002, the film received a deserved Academy Award nomination for Best Animated Feature.

Back in the world of hard reality, Diaz took part in the charity telethon *America: A Tribute to Heroes*, the American entertainment industry's response to the 11 September terrorist attacks. The celebrity cast for this event included fellow film stars Tom Cruise, Julia Roberts, Mark Wahlberg, Goldie Hawn, Kurt Russell and Clint Eastwood. There were also appearances from singers Billy Joel, Tom Petty and Mariah Carey, and super-model Cindy Crawford. Standing next to *Charlie's Angels* costar Lucy Liu, Diaz formed part of the celebrity backdrop to Willie Nelson's performance of 'America the Beautiful'. While some observers felt that *A Tribute to Heroes* was in questionable taste, the show raised over $150 million. On 20 September 2001, Diaz was honoured at the eighth annual Women in Hollywood gala.

Vanilla Sky (2001) could be viewed as a bold, unconventional attempt at a mainstream 'art' film. Or just a self-indulgent vanity project that reeks of pretension and half-arsed symbolism. Producer-star Tom Cruise, Hollywood's biggest box-office draw, obviously wanted to extend his range as A Serious Actor. Writer-director Cameron Crowe had a proven commercial track record, as the man behind the hits *Jerry Maguire* (1996), starring Cruise, and *Almost Famous* (2000). *Vanilla Sky* is a remake of *Abre los ojos* (*Open Your Eyes*, 1997), directed, co-written and co-scored by Alejandro Amenábar. This Spanish-French-Italian co-production drew international acclaim, offering a stylish, assured blend of romantic thriller, *film noir*, science fiction and nightmare fantasy. In truth, *Open Your Eyes* has been over-hyped, yet it's original, intriguing and tautly plotted.

Both Crowe and Cruise were big fans of Amenábar's film and wanted to stay faithful to the original movie, retaining all the key scenes while adding new elements. Crowe described *Vanilla Sky* as the 'rock cover version' of the 'acoustic' *Open Your Eyes*. However honourable the intentions, the end result misfired. In contrast to its inspiration, Crowe's bastardised remix is clumsy, confusing and unengaging. The 'twist' ending is one of the lamest tricks in the storytelling book. According to Crowe, *Vanilla Sky* was partly inspired by Elvis Presley. If the King is still alive, he should sue.

Financed by Paramount, filming for *Vanilla Sky* began on 6 November 2000. The $68 million budget, unusually modest for a Tom Cruise movie, reflected the material's non-mainstream nature. Faced with an impending Actors' and Writers' Guild strike (which in the event never materialised), Crowe and his team were under pressure to work fast. Crowe felt that the "adrenalised" nature of the production helped him capture the "urgency" of the material. It could be argued that the hastily written script and rushed shoot only magnified the flaws in an already ill-conceived project. Crowe finished production on 19 March 2001, just over four months later.

Cameron Diaz agreed to play the supporting role of Cruise's discarded lover, whose suicidal behaviour sets the plot in motion. Diaz had been interested in playing Cruise's girlfriend in *Jerry Maguire*. On that occasion, Cameron

Above: *Julie Gianni lures ex-lover David Aames (Tom Cruise) into her car in* Vanilla Sky. *It's going to be a bumpy ride.*

Crowe decided she wasn't right for the part of plucky single mother Dorothy Boyd. The role went to the relatively unknown Rene Zellweger, who scored highly on the cute factor.

Spanish actress Penélope Cruz, who'd co-starred in *Open Your Eyes*, reprised her original role, playing Cruise's enigmatic new girl-friend. While their screen romance proved largely illusory, Cruise and Cruz fell for each other during production on the film. The resulting tabloid frenzy created a whole new level of interest in *Vanilla Sky*. Cruise's wife, Nicole Kidman, had recently starred in Alejandro Amenábar's first English-language film, *The Others* (2001), a highly successful ghost story. Cruise served as an executive producer on the movie. Perhaps he should have limited his association with the Spanish writer-director to this one, original film.

Marketed as an 'erotic thriller', *Vanilla Sky* doesn't play either element to great effect. Like *Head Above Water*, the film offers damning proof that Hollywood remakes of foreign originals are generally a bad idea. The new title refers to the clouds in a Monet painting inherited by the main character from his late mother. According to Cameron Crowe: "Vanilla Sky is a feeling, a state of mind, a dream of a life that may or may not actually exist." In fact, *Vanilla Sky* was the original

title of Crowe's previous film, *Almost Famous*, and the director didn't want to waste it.

Tom Cruise stars as David Aames, spoiled heir to a New York magazine empire. A multi-millionaire with the world at his feet, this hedonistic, self-centred playboy uses people up and throws them away. One of Aames' friends describes new lover Julie Gianni (Diaz) as a "fuck buddy". Aames denies this, yet casually dumps her at his birthday party after taking a peek at sultry, sizzling Sofia Serrano (Cruz). Sofia is a gifted dancer and part-time dental assistant. Julie appears to be some kind of actress or singer or model, who keeps missing auditions. There's no real contest. The fact that Sofia is already going out with Aames' best friend isn't a problem. Still, David shows his essential decency by not sleeping with her on their first night together.

Aames gets his much-deserved comeuppance early on in the film. Facially disfigured in a car smash caused by the vengeful Julie, he must wear a latex mask, or 'aesthetic regenerative shield', to cover his now hideous features. The end result is an unlikely cross between the Phantom of the Opera and the Hunchback of Notre Dame. In one unforgettable scene Aames shuffles along a corridor, crying out for "tech support!" Crowe claimed that he wanted Tom Cruise to give "a big and boldly modern performance". Most viewers would use a different description. In fairness, Cruise held his own in Stanley Kubrick's similarly disorientating and shallow *Eyes Wide Shut* (1999). He also played a memorably unsympathetic character in Paul Thomas Anderson's epic suburban satire *Magnolia* (1999). On the other hand, neither of these films called for him

do a drunken dance routine.

The post-car wreck scenes could be reality, or Aames' dream, or a taste of the afterlife. There's nothing in *Vanilla Sky* to make anyone care either way. Aames wakes up next to Sofia one day, then finds himself in bed with Brenda, supposedly dead, the next. Are they in fact the same person? He is arrested for murder, but the police won't divulge the identity of the victim. Is Aames' despised board of directors conspiring against him?

Allowed minimal screen time, Diaz gives the best performance by a long way, though her on-screen orgasm lacks conviction. Julie Gianni is the only character to display human feelings, her yearning and disappointment turned to frustrated rage.

Nuria (Najwa Nimri), the equivalent character in *Open Your Eyes*, is largely unsympathetic. Outfitted in a symbolic red dress, this black-haired, pill-popping *femme fatale* is little more than a plot device. *Vanilla Sky* gives Julie more dialogue and more depth, Crowe's one improvement on the original film. (Though some of her expanded dialogue is pretty ill-advised; at one point, she utters the immortal line: "I swallowed your cum. That means something.") Sofia Serrano, wise beyond her years, sums up Julie perfectly: "…the loneliest girl to ever hold a martini". Whether posing seductively in a duvet or drunkenly slow-dancing with a wine waiter, Julie has an air of desperation about her. No matter how many times she screws Aames, he is out of her league as a long-term prospect.

Cast aside by Aames as a meaningless one-night stand, she protests at his lack of commitment: "When you sleep with someone, your body makes a promise, even if you don't." Not in New York, it seems. If nothing else, Julie's sad death is an awful warning against driving in high heels. At one point, 'ghost' Julie gives

its opening weekend. This was enough to give the film the number one spot at the box-office, dislodging the high-profile *Ocean's 11* remake. The reviews were generally poor, the *Wall Street Journal* arguing that "Its tone is unquenchably pretentious and its scale is overblown." *Vanilla Sky* opened in Britain on 25 January 2002, where the negative reviews easily outweighed the raves. *Guardian* critic Peter Bradshaw dismissed the film as "an extraordinarily narcissistic high-concept vanity project for producer-star Tom Cruise… a cumbersome and bombastic film, lumbered with pseudo-futuristic ideas." Once again, *Vanilla Sky* took the number one spot during its opening weekend, making nearly £3 million.

While the Tom Cruise-Penélope Cruz factor helped *Vanilla Sky* off to a solid start in both territories, public interest soon waned. After four weeks on release in the US, the film's total box-office gross stood at $81 million. Though hardly disastrous, this was a long way from blockbuster status, consigning the film to the number six spot. By contrast, *Ocean's 11*, still at number three in the charts, had earned $152 million. A couple of weeks later, *Vanilla Sky* dropped out of the top ten. In Britain, the film managed two weekends at number one before being displaced by the Disney-Pixar smash hit *Monsters Inc.* (2001).

Initially touted as surefire Academy Award material, *Vanilla Sky* soon stalled as a serious Oscar contender, netting just one minor nomination for Best Song. Diaz received a 2002 American Film Institute nomination for Featured Actor of the Year – Female. Diaz also picked up another Golden Globe nomination, for Best Supporting

Left: At the Vanilla Sky premiere, in December 2001.

Aames a good kicking. He had it coming.

By contrast, Tom Cruise's trademark smirks and less 'endearing' screams are ludicrous. Penélope Cruz, working from a dud script in a – for her – foreign language, seems to be struggling. Cruz looks far more comfortable in *Open Your Eyes*, despite having to perform as a mime artist. The supporting cast, which includes Kurt Russell, Tilda Swinton and Timothy Spall, do what they can. Cast as Cruise's psychiatrist, Russell looks understandably perplexed. Producer-director Stacy Title, who worked with Diaz on *The Last Supper* and *Feeling Minnesota*, appears in a bit part.

Sold with the tiresomely 'enigmatic' tagline 'LoveHateDreamsLifeWorkPlayFriendshipSex', *Vanilla Sky* hit American multiplex screens on 14 December 2001, grossing $25 million over

Above: *Shooting the troubled* Gangs of New York *in January 2001.*

Actress, losing out to Jennifer Connelly. Having beaten Diaz to the lead in *Waking the Dead*, Connelly triumphed once again, taking the award for her performance opposite Russell Crowe in *A Beautiful Mind* (2001).

Diaz made a rare excursion into period drama with *Gangs of New York* (2002). This eagerly awaited German-Italian-American co-production teamed her with Leonardo DiCaprio and top director Martin Scorsese. *Gangs* is set between 1846 and 1863, the Tammany Hall era when New York was rife with political corruption. The film deals with the violent conflict between the newly arrived Italian immigrants and the Anglo Saxon 'natives' already established in the fast-growing city.

Leonardo DiCaprio made a name for himself in offbeat movies like *The Basketball Diaries* (1995) and *The Quick and the Dead* (1995). He then earned teen heart-throb status with his performances in Baz Luhrmann's *William Shakespeare's Romeo + Juliet* (1996) and James Cameron's Oscar-laden blockbuster *Titanic* (1997). DiCaprio attempted to lose this new image with *The Beach* (2000), a downbeat drama made by the British team behind *Trainspotting* and *A Life Less Ordinary*. A big fan of Martin Scorsese, the star signed on for *Gangs of New York* back in February 1999, long before production started. One of America's finest living directors, Scorsese's most recent credits were the atypical *Kundun* (1997), a biopic of the Dalai Lama, and *Bringing Out the Dead* (1999), a New York tale of half-crazed ambulance drivers.

Based on a book by Herbert Asbury, the script for *Gangs of New York* was by Jay Cocks,

a veteran film critic, Kenneth Lonergan and Steven Zaillian, who delivered the final draft. Zaillian's previous credits included *Schindler's List* (1993), for which he won an Academy Award, and the more lightweight *Mission: Impossible* (1996). *Gangs of New York* centres on the lethal rivalry between two gangs, the Dead Rabbits and the Native Americans. DiCaprio stars as Amsterdam Vallon, a young man seeking vengeance for the murder of his father, the Rabbits' leader. A formidable mobster in his own right, Vallon eventually took control of the New York gangs and ended the Irish-Italian conflict.

The supporting cast for *Gangs* includes Liam Neeson, playing DiCaprio's father, Jim Broadbent, Brendan Gleeson and Daniel Day-Lewis. Day-Lewis had starred in Scorsese's more genteel period drama *The Age of Innocence* (1993), set in 1870s New York. This time around, he takes the showy supporting role of Bill 'The Butcher' Poole, boss of the Native Americans. Vallon holds Poole responsible for his father's death, making a showdown inevitable. Scorsese originally wanted regular star Robert De Niro to play Poole. Day-Lewis made for an intriguing, if unlikely, replacement.

A relative latecomer to the production,

Left: On location in Rome with Leonardo DiCaprio, shooting Gangs of New York.

Diaz co-stars as Jenny, a young thief who falls for Vallon. British actress Anna Friel was originally cast in the role, and actually began shooting on *Gangs* in Italy. As Friel explained to *Guardian* journalist Stuart Jeffries: "I worked on the film for one day and then the producers called and said, 'Cameron wants to do it.'" Realistic about the Hollywood system, Friel graciously stepped aside, holding no personal grudge against Diaz: "I could understand... I'd have chosen her."

Budgeted at $90 million, *Gangs of New York* began filming on 30 August 2000 at the Cinecittá studios in Rome. Despite the talent both in front of and behind the camera, the production had struggled to attract the necessary finance. At the last minute, the American company Miramax, based in New York, stepped in to buy up the US distribution rights and keep the film afloat. The Italian locations included Lazio, probably best known internationally for its football team. While Anna Friel's dismissal provided some copy for the press, the latter were more interested in the alleged misbehaviour of Leonardo DiCaprio. According to media reports, the

star embraced the famed Italian night-life a little too enthusiastically. Turning up on set the next day, hours late and in no state to work, DiCaprio received a very public telling-off from Scorsese. Once the Italian scenes were completed, the production relocated to New York City. In total, shooting lasted nearly six months, wrapping in February 2001.

Originally set for release in late 2001, *Gangs of New York* was pushed back to mid-2002 in response to the 11 September terrorist attacks on New York City and Washington DC. Along with several other Hollywood productions featuring violence and destruction in urban America, *Gangs* seemed an inappropriate movie to unleash on a still shell-shocked public. Despite the period setting, scenes of New York being torn apart by gang warfare were too close to recent events. By contrast, more gung-ho films like *Behind Enemy Lines* (2001) and *Black Hawk Down* (2002), which celebrated American military tenacity and personal courage in foreign war zones, had their releases brought forward. Over the summer of 2002, reports emerged that *Gangs of New York* was beset by bitter

post-production wrangles. The film was still not finished as this book went to press.

Probably in need of some light relief, Diaz agreed to make a cameo appearance in the high school comedy *Slackers* (2002), a low-brow effort aimed squarely at teenage boys. Directed by Dewey Nicks from a script by David H Steinberg, the film starred Devon Sawa, Jason Segel and Michael Maronna, none of them exactly household names. The plot, as such, involves grade fraud, blackmail by geek (Jason Schwartzman) and the choice between true love and easy graduation. *Slackers* hints at venturing into harder, darker territory than the average teen comedy, playing the nerd character as a borderline psychopath. Most of the time, however, the movie throws in the usual flatulence jokes and the odd topless grandmother (an obvious steal from *There's Something About Mary*). Cast as 'Herself', Diaz lends the production a brief touch of class.

Promoted with the uninspired slogan: 'Higher Education Just Hit A New Low', *Slackers* opened in the United States on 1 February 2002. This date suggested that the film's distributors didn't have much faith in their product, its first weekend on release coinciding with the American Football Super Bowl on Sunday 3 February, when most Americans are glued to their television sets for the big game. Diaz aside, they didn't miss much.

Diaz returned to top-billed leading roles with *The Sweetest Thing* (2002), a romantic comedy produced by Columbia Pictures, who'd done very well out of *Charlie's Angels*. In terms of Diaz's star status, the most significant aspect of this film was her $15 million fee. This put Diaz in the same league as Jodie Foster, Meg

Above: *Christina Walters takes time off from her manhunt in* The Sweetest Thing.

Ryan, and her fellow Angel Drew Barrymore, pretty good company. By comparison, Sandra Bullock and Jennifer Lopez were taking home $12 million per film, while Michelle Pfeiffer, Angelina Jolie, Meryl Streep and Gwyneth Paltrow had to make do with $10 million. Only Julia Roberts, Diaz's co-star from *My Best Friend's Wedding*, could command a higher fee, receiving $20 million for *Erin Brockovich*. Diaz would soon make up the difference.

The Sweetest Thing was directed by Roger Kumble, a long-time associate of Peter and Bobby Farrelly. Kumble's uncredited work on the screenplay for *There's Something About*

Left: *Christina Walters hangs with the girls in The Sweetest Thing.*

Mary earned him a special 'thanks' at the end of the film. On his own, Kumble had scored a hit as the writer-director of *Cruel Intentions* (1999). This jet-black update of *Dangerous Liaisons* provided a major change of pace for wholesome *Buffy the Vampire Slayer* star Sarah Michelle Gellar, here cast as a cruel teen temptress. For *The Sweetest Thing*, Kumble worked from a screenplay by Nancy Pimental. A former stand-up comedian specialising in improvisation, Pimenthal broke into television as a writer for the animated series *South Park*, which easily matched the Farrelly Brothers for gross-out humour. *Sweetest Thing* was Pimenthal's first feature film script.

Cameron Diaz starred as Christina Walters, a dedicated night-clubber with a fear of commitment. When Christina finally meets the man of her dreams, she must learn how to woo the opposite sex. The part of Christina's elusive boyfriend went to Thomas Jane, who'd appeared in *Magnolia* and *Deep Blue Sea* (1999), a tale of genetically modified sharks. (It could happen.) The supporting cast included Parker Posey, *Cruel Intentions*

co-star Selma Blair and Christina Applegate. Well-known for her role in the hit television sit-com *Married... with Children*, Applegate took the part of Diaz's supportive best friend. *Sweetest Thing* began filming on 2 April 2001, shortly after Diaz finished shooting *Gangs of New York*, wrapping on 15 June. The film opened in the United States on 29 March 2002, British viewers waiting until 7 June. And if she needed any reminder of her star status, Diaz was made the subject of a 2001 television profile, *Headliners and Legends: Cameron Diaz*, directed by Sienna McLean.

With *Charlie's Angels 2* in the bag, along with the $20 million payday, Cameron Diaz could well afford to pick and choose her film projects. In February 2002, she agreed to co-star opposite Michael Keaton in the black comedy *Going Mad in Hollywood*. Set during the 1960s, the film follows the progress of a British screenwriter from Soho to Cannes to Los Angeles. As *Invisible Circus* demonstrated, Diaz seems to have a particular affinity for the sixties. Michael Keaton is probably best known for his work with director Tim Burton on *Beetlejuice*

(1988), *Batman* (1989) and *Batman Returns* (1992). Since hanging up the Batsuit, Keaton's Hollywood profile had dropped a little. He'd taken a supporting role in Quentin Tarantino's eagerly awaited *Jackie Brown* (1997), which didn't boost his career the way *Pulp Fiction* had revived John Travolta's. Keaton then played the lead in the sickly sentimental *Jack Frost* (1998), the kind of movie that gives wholesome family entertainment a bad name. Along with Diaz, Michael Keaton had been part of the celebrity line-up for *America: A Tribute to Heroes*.

Despite its title, *Going Mad in Hollywood* was a largely British production, directed by Michael Winterbottom from a screenplay by David Sherwin. Winterbottom specialised in intense, often downbeat dramas about frustrated relationships. Since his debut with the odd *Butterfly Kiss* (1995), he'd directed *Jude* (1996), *Welcome to Sarajevo* (1997), *With or Without You* (1999) and *24 Hour Party People* (2002), among others. *Jude*, *With or Without You* and *24 Hour Party People* all co-starred Christopher Eccleston, who'd worked with Diaz on *Invisible Circus*. David Sherwin's film career dated back to the 1960s, when he provided the screenplay for director Lindsay Anderson's surreal satire *If ....* (1968). Sherwin and Anderson later reunited for *O Lucky Man!* (1973) and *Britannia Hospital* (1982). For *Going Mad in Hollywood*, Sherwin adapted his own bestselling novel.

Eight years after her debut in *The Mask*, Cameron Diaz's Hollywood future looks assured. For someone who broke into movies with zero knowledge of either acting or the film industry, she's enjoyed an extraordinary rise to the top.

Without the benefit of hindsight, most of Diaz's early career choices look hopelessly misguided. Few budding stars would choose to follow a smash hit Jim Carrey comedy with five 'indie' films in a row. Playing second fiddle to Julia Roberts in *My Best Friend's Wedding* could easily have backfired, with Diaz lost in the blaze of Roberts' 'comeback' performance. As for *There's Something About Mary*, how many non-porn stars would even consider a role that involves handling their co-star's sperm? Cameron Diaz has never been afraid to take risks.

On top of her *Charlie's Angels 2* deal, Diaz will earn an estimated $10 million to reprise the part of Fiona in *Shrek 2*, due in 2004. This is nearly seven times her fee for the first film. Not a bad rate of pay for one week's work in a recording studio.

Of course, nothing is certain in an industry where stardom is often fleeting and there are few leading roles for women over 40. Diaz has yet to suffer an expensive, high-profile commercial flop, the most serious test of a star's long-term staying power. The $20 million fee for the *Charlie's Angels* sequel may prove a one-off, though Diaz will probably remain among the highest paid Hollywood stars. For the time being.

That said, she seems just as happy working on offbeat, low-budget movies for a fraction of her usual price. While many stars cultivate an established, reassuringly constant screen persona, Cameron Diaz just wants to play interesting and fun roles. And who's complaining?

filmography

THE MASK
New Line/Dark Horse • 1994 • 101 minutes

Executive producers: Michael De Luca, Mike Richardson, Charles Russell; Associate producers: Ann Burgund, Carla Fry; Producer: Robert Engelman; Director: Charles Russell; Screenplay: Mike Werb (based on a story by Michael Fallon and Mark Verheiden); Director of photography: John R Leonetti; Editing: Arthur Coburn; Production design: Craig Stearns; Music: Randy Edelman; Creator special make-up: Greg Cannom.
Cast: Jim Carrey (Stanley Ipkiss/ The Mask), Cameron Diaz (Tina Carlyle), Peter Riegert (Lieutenant Mitch Kellaway), Peter Greene (Dorian Tyrrell), Richard Jeni (Charlie Schumaker), Amy Yasbeck (Peggy Brandt).

THE LAST SUPPER
Electric/Vault • 1995 • 91 minutes

Executive producer: David Cooper; Co-executive producers: Stacy Title, Jonathan Penner; Producers: Matt Cooper, Larry Weinberg; Co-producers: Lori Miller, Dan Rosen; Associate producer: Luis Colina; Director: Stacy Title; Screenplay: Dan Rosen; Director of photography: Paul Cameron; Editing: Luis Colina; Production design: Linda Burton; Original music: Mark Mothersbaugh.

Cast: Cameron Diaz (Jude), Ron Eldard (Pete), Annabeth Gish (Paulie), Jonathan Penner (Marc), Courtney B Vance (Luke), Jason Alexander (the Anti-Environmentalist), Nora Dunn (Sheriff Alice Stanley), Charles Durning (Reverend Gerald Hutchens), Bryn Erin (Heather), Mark Harmon (Dominant Male), Ron Perlman (Norman Arbuthnot), Bill Paxton (Zachary Cody), Carly Weber (young Jude) [role cut from release print].

SHE'S THE ONE
Twentieth Century Fox/Good Machine/ Marlboro • 1996 • 96 minutes

Executive producers: Michael Nozik, Robert Redford; Co-executive producer: John Sloss, Producers: Edward Burns, Ted Hope, James Schamus; Director: Edward Burns; Screenplay: Edward Burns; Director of photography: Frank Prinzi; Editing: Susan Graef; Production design: William Barclay; Music: Tom Petty.
Cast: Edward Burns (Mickey Fitzpatrick), Mike McGlone (Francis Fitzpatrick), John Mahoney (Mr Fitzpatrick), Jennifer Aniston (Renee Fitzpatrick), Maxine Bahns (Hope Fitzpatrick), Cameron Diaz (Heather Davis), Malachy McCourt (Tom), Leslie Mann (Connie), Tom Tammi (Father John).

FEELING MINNESOTA
New Line/Jersey Films • 1996 • 99 minutes

Executive producer: Erwin Stoff; Producers: Danny DeVito, Michael Shamberg, Stacey Sher; Co-producer: Eric McLeod; Associate producer: Carla Macy; Director: Steven Baigelman; Screenplay: Steven Baigelman; Director of photography: Walt Lloyd; Editing: Martin Walsh; Production design: Naomi Shohan; Original music: Chris Cornell, Los Lobos.
Cast: Keanu Reeves (Jjaks Clayton), Cameron Diaz (Freddie Clayton), Vincent D'Onofrio (Sam Clayton), Delroy Lindo (Red), Dan Aykroyd (Ben Costikyan), Courtney Love (Rhonda), Tuesday Weld (Norma Clayton), Levon Helm (Bible salesman).

HEAD ABOVE WATER
Warner/Head Above Water/Firmjewel/ InterMedia/Fine Line • 1996 • 92 minutes

Executive producers: Guy East, Tristan Whalley; Producers: John M Jacobsen, Jim Wilson; Co-producer: Helen Pollak; Associate producers: Maria M Machado, Lynne Whiteford; Director: Jim Wilson; Screenplay: Theresa Marie (based on the film *Hoden over Vannet*, by Eirik Ildahl and Geir Eriksen); Director of

Right: Diaz attends the premiere of Being John Malkovich at the Venice Film Festival in 1999.

photography: Richard Bowen;
Editing: Michael R Miller;
Production design: Jeffrey Beecroft;
Music: Christopher Young.
Cast: Harvey Keitel (George),
Cameron Diaz (Nathalie), Craig
Sheffer (Lance), Billy Zane (Kent),
Shay Duffin (policeman).

KEYS TO TULSA

Polygram/ITC/Peyton/Empire • 1997 •
114 minutes

Executive producers: Michael
Birnbaum, Peter Isacksen; Producers:
Leslie Greif, Harley Peyton; Co-pro-
ducer: Guy J Louthan; Associate
producers: David Gaines, Kenny
Golde; Director: Leslie Greif;
Screenplay: Harley Peyton (based on
the novel by Brian Fair Berkey);
Director of photography: Robert
Fraisse; Editing: Eric L Beason,
Louis F Cioffi, Michael R Miller;
Production design: Derek R Hill;
Music: Stephen Endelman.
Cast: Eric Stoltz (Richter Boudreau),
James Spader (Ronnie Stover),
Deborah Kara Unger (Vicky Michaels
Stover), Michael Rooker (Keith
Michaels), Mary Tyler Moore
(Cynthia Boudreau), James Coburn
(Harmon Shaw), Peter Strauss (Chip
Carlson), Cameron Diaz (Trudy).

MY BEST FRIEND'S WEDDING

Columbia TriStar/Predawn • 1997 •
105 minutes

Executive producers: Gil Netter,
Patricia Whitcher; Producers: Ronald
Bass, Jerry Zucker; Associate produc-
ers: Patricia Cullen, Bill Johnson;
Director: P J Hogan; Screenplay:
Ronald Bass; Director of photogra-
phy: Laszlo Kovacs; Editing: Garth
Craven, Lisa Fruchtman; Production
design: Richard Sylbert; Original
music: James Newton Howard, Burt
Bacharach (songs).
Cast: Julia Roberts (Julianne Potter),
Dermot Mulroney (Michael O'Neal),
Cameron Diaz (Kimberly Wallace),
Rupert Everett (George Downes),
Philip Bosco (Walter Wallace), M
Emmet Walsh (Joe O'Neal), Rachel
Griffiths (Samantha Newhouse),
Carrie Preston (Mandy Newhouse),
Susan Sullivan (Isabelle Wallace),
Harry Shearer (Jonathan P F Ritt).

A LIFE LESS ORDINARY

Polygram/Figment • 1997 • 102 minutes

Producer: Andrew Macdonald;
Director: Danny Boyle; Screenplay:
John Hodge; Director of photography:
Brian Tufano; Editing: Masahiro
Hirakubo; Production design: Kave
Quinn; Original music: David Arnold;
Animation producer: Sophie Byrne.

Cast: Ewan McGregor (Robert
Lewis), Cameron Diaz (Celine
Naville), Holly Hunter (O'Reilly),
Delroy Lindo (Jackson), Dan Hedaya
(Gabriel), Ian McNeice (Mayhew),
Stanley Tucci (Elliot Zweikel), Ian
Holm (Naville), Maury Chaykin
(Tod), Judith Ivey (Celine's mother).

FEAR AND LOATHING IN LAS VEGAS

Universal/Rhino • 1998 • 118 minutes

Executive producers: Harold
Bronson, Richard Foos; Producers:
Patrick Cassavetti, Laila Nabulsi,
Stephen Nemeth; Co-producer: Elliot
Lewis Rosenblatt; Associate producer:
John Jergens; Director: Terry Gilliam;
Screenplay: Terry Gilliam, Tony
Grisoni, Tod Davies, Alex Cox (based
on the book by Hunter S
Thompson); Director of photogra-
phy: Nicola Pecorini; Editing: Lesley
Walker; Production design: Alex
McDowell; Original music: Ray
Cooper, Michael Kamen.
Cast: Johnny Depp (Raoul Duke),
Benicio Del Toro (Dr Gonzo), Tobey
Maguire (hitchhiker), Ellen Barkin
(waitress at North Star Café), Gary
Busey (highway patrolman),
Christina Ricci (Lucy), Mark
Harmon (magazine reporter at Mint
400), Cameron Diaz (blonde TV
reporter), Katherine Helmond (desk
clerk at Mint Hotel), Penn Jillette

(barker at Bazooko Circus), Lyle Lovett (road person), Flea (musician in Matrix Club Men's Room), Harry Dean Stanton (Judge), Hunter S Thompson (Old Uncle Duke).

THERE'S SOMETHING ABOUT MARY

Twentieth Century Fox • 1998 • 119 minutes

Executive producers: Bobby Farrelly, Peter Farrelly; Producers: Frank Beddor, Michael Steinberg, Bradley Thomas, Charles B Wessler; Co-producers: Marc S Fischer, James B Rogers; Associate producers: Mark Charpentier, Patrick Healy; Directors: Bobby Farrelly, Peter Farrelly; Screenplay: Ed Decter, John J Strauss, Peter Farrelly, Bobby Farrelly (based on a story by Ed Decter and John J Strauss); Director of photography: Mark Irwin; Editing: Christopher Greenbury; Art direction: Arlan Jay Vetter; Original music: Jonathan Richman.
Cast: Cameron Diaz (Mary Jensen Matthews), Matt Dillon (Pat Healy), Ben Stiller (Ted Stroehmann), Lee Evans (Norman Phipps/Tucker), Chris Elliott (Dom Woganowski), Lin Shaye (Magda), Jeffrey Tambor (Sully), Markie Post (Sheila Jensen), Keith David (Charlie Jensen), W Earl Brown (Warren Jensen), Hillary Matthews (Mrs Woganowski), Brett

Favre (himself), Jonathan Richman (Jonathan), Emilio Diaz (jailbird).

VERY BAD THINGS

Polygram/Initial Entertainment/Interscope/ BallPark/Universal • 1998 • 100 minutes

Executive producers: Ted Field, Michael A Helfant, Scott Kroopf, Christian Slater; Producers: Cindy Cowan, Diane Nabatoff, Michael Schiffer; Director: Peter Berg; Screenplay: Peter Berg; Director of photography: David Hennings; Editing: Dan Lebental; Production design: Dina Lipton; Music: Stewart Copeland.
Cast: Christian Slater (Robert Boyd), Cameron Diaz (Laura Garrety), Jon Favreau (Kyle Fisher), Leland Orser (Charles Moore), Daniel Stern (Adam Berkow), Jeremy Piven (Michael Berkow), Jeanne Tripplehorn (Lois Berkow), Kobe Tai [as 'Carla Scott'] (Tina).

MAN WOMAN FILM

Advanced Order Systems/Canis Lupus Entertainment • 1999 • 83 minutes

Producer: Cameron Pearson; Co-producer: Henri Falconi; Associate producers: Jimmy Franklin, Charles E Wall; Director: Cameron Pearson; Screenplay: Cameron Pearson; Director of photography: Eric Grush;

Editing: Cameron Pearson.
Cast: Steve Abee (frustrated café poet), Lee Arenberg (Ali), Matt Baxter (Cyrus), Gavin Bellour (Kurtz: rapist of mannequins), Jessica Beshir (Ali's girl), Bernadette Colomine (French director), Cameron Diaz (random celebrity), Leslie Doe (Crispian's assistant), Henri Falconi (Juan Cocteau), Chris Figgler (man in a dress), Jimmy Franklin (anti-James Mason), Anel Lopez Gorham (Harper Lee), Anna Khaja (Anastasia X), Christopher Metas (Gestapo mime and sex cult freak), Elly Nesis (squealing mime), Brendon O'Malley (Hartbroken frenchman), Paolerico (mime/drummer), Cameron Pearson (Cruz), Ian Stevens (Ariel Treplev Potter), Rachel Stolte (Bassist), Atticus Travis (Boy), Charles E Wall (Crispian Belfridge), Grant Walpole (Rupert).

BEING JOHN MALKOVICH

Polygram/Gramercy/Single Cell/ Propaganda/Universal • 1999 • 113 minutes

Executive producers: Charlie Kaufman, Michael Kuhn, Producers: Steve Golin, Vincent Landay, Sandy Stern, Michael Stipe; Director: Spike Jonze; Screenplay: Charlie Kaufman; Director of photography: Lance Acord; Editing: Eric Zumbrunnen; Production design: K K Barrett; Music: Carter Burwell.
Cast: John Cusack (Craig Schwartz),

Cameron Diaz (Lotte Schwartz), Catherine Keener (Maxine), John Malkovich (John Horatio Malkovich), Orson Bean (Dr Lester), Mary Kay Place (Floris), W Earl Brown (first JM Inc customer), Charlie Sheen (Charlie), Winona Ryder (herself), David Fincher (Christopher Bing) [uncredited], Sean Penn (himself) [uncredited].

ANY GIVEN SUNDAY

Warner/Ixtlan/The Donners' Co • 1999 • 162 minutes (US theatrical version)/150 minutes (international version)

Executive producers: Richard Donner, Oliver Stone; Producers: Dan Halsted, Lauren Shuler Donner, Clayton Townsend; Co-producers: Eric Hamburg, Jonathan Krauss, Richard Rutowski; Director: Oliver Stone; Screenplay: John Logan, Oliver Stone (based on a story by Daniel Pyne and John Logan); Director of photography: Salvatore Totino; Editing: Stuart Levy, Thomas J Nordberg, Keith Salmon, Stuart Waks; Production design: Victor Kempster; Music: Richard Horowitz, Paul Kelly, Robbie Robertson.
Cast: Al Pacino (Tony D'Amato), Cameron Diaz (Christina Pagniacci), Dennis Quaid (Jack 'Cap' Rooney), James Woods (Dr Harvey Mandrake), Jamie Foxx (Willie Beamen), LL Cool J (Julian Washington), Matthew Modine (Dr Ollie Powers), Jim

Brown (Montezuma Monroe), Lauren Holly (Cindy Rooney), Ann-Margret (Margaret Pagniacci), Elizabeth Berkley (Mandy), Charlton Heston (Commissioner).

THINGS YOU CAN TELL JUST BY LOOKING AT HER

MGM/UA • 2000 • 80 minutes

Executive producer: Elie Samaha, Andrew Stevens; Producers: Jon Avnet, Lisa Lindstrom, Marsha Oglesby; Director: Rodrigo Garcia; Screenplay: Rodrigo Garcia; Director of photography: Emmanuel Lubezki; Editing: Amy E Duddleston; Production design: Jerry Fleming; Music: Edward Shearmur.
Cast: Glenn Close (Dr Elaine Keener), Cameron Diaz (Carol), Calista Flockhart (Christine Taylor), Kathy Baker (Rose), Amy Brenneman (Kathy), Holly Hunter (Rebecca), Gregory Hines (Robert).

CHARLIE'S ANGELS

Columbia/Flower Films • 2000 • 98 minutes

Executive producers: Joseph M. Caracciolo, Aaron Spelling, Betty Thomas, Jenno Topping; Producers: Drew Barrymore, Leonard Goldberg, Nancy Juvonen; Associate producer: Amanda Goldberg; Director: McG;

Screenplay: Ryan Rowe, Ed Solomon, John August (based on the television series created by Ivan Goff and Ben Roberts); Directors of photography: Russell Carpenter, Michael St Hilaire; Editing: Peter Teschner, Wayne Wahrman; Production design: Michael Riva; Songs: Bootsy Collins, Tom Hamilton, Michael Jackson, Joey Kramer, Joe Perry, Edward Shearmur, Fatboy Slim, Steven Tyler, Brad Whitford.
Cast: Cameron Diaz (Natalie Cook), Drew Barrymore (Dylan Sanders), Lucy Liu (Alex Munday), Bill Murray (John Bosley), Sam Rockwell (Eric Knox), Kelly Lynch (Vivian Wood), Tim Curry (Roger Corwin), Crispin Glover (The Thin Man), Luke Wilson (Pete), John Forsythe (Charles Townsend [voice]), Matt LeBlanc (Jason Gibbons), Tom Green (Chad).

THE INVISIBLE CIRCUS

New Line • 2001 • 92 minutes

Executive producers: Arianna C. Bocco, Tim Van Rellim; Producers: Julia Chasman, Nick Wechsler; Director: Adam Brooks; Screenplay: Adam Brooks (based on the novel by Jennifer Egan); Director of photography: Henry Braham; Editing: Elizabeth Kling; Production design: Robin Standefer; Music: Nick Laird-Clowes.
Cast: Cameron Diaz (Faith), Jordana Brewster (Phoebe), Christopher

Eccleston (Wolf), Blythe Danner (Gail), Patrick Bergin (Gene), Moritz Bleibtreu (Eric).

SHREK
PDI-Dreamworks • 2001 • 90 minutes

Executive producers: Penney Finkelman Cox, Sandra Rabins, Steven Spielberg [uncredited]; Co-executive producer: David Lipman; Producers: Jeffrey Katzenberg, Aron Warner, John H Williams; Co-producers: Ted Elliott, Terry Rossio; Directors: Andrew Adamson, Vicky Jenson; Screenplay: Ted Elliott, Terry Rossio, Joe Stillman, Roger S H Schulman (based on the book by William Steig); Additional dialogue: Cody Cameron, Chris Miller, Conrad Vernon; Editing: Sim Evan-Jones; Production design: James Hegedus; Original music: Harry Gregson-Williams, John Powell; Additional music: James McKee Smith.
Voice cast: Mike Myers (Shrek), Eddie Murphy (Duncan the Donkey), Cameron Diaz (Princess Fiona), John Lithgow (Lord Farquaad of Duloc), Vincent Cassel (Monsieur Robin Hoo), Mike Myers (blind mouse).

VANILLA SKY
Paramount • 2001 • 135 minutes

Executive producers: Bill Block, Fernando Bovaira; Danny Bramson, Jonathan Sanger, Patrick Wachsberger; Producers: Cameron Crowe, Tom Cruise, Paula Wagner; Co-producer: Donald J Lee Jr.; Associate producers: Michael Doven, Scott M Martin; Director: Cameron Crowe, Screenplay: Cameron Crowe (based on the film *Abre los ojos*, by Alejandro Amenábar and Mateo Gil Rodriguez); Director of photography: John Toll; Editing: Joe Hutshing, Mark Livolsi; Production design: Catherine Hardwicke; Original music: Nancy Wilson.
Cast: Tom Cruise (David Aames), Penélope Cruz (Sofia Serrano), Cameron Diaz (Julie Gianni), Kurt Russell (McCabe), Jason Lee (Brian Shelby), Noah Taylor (Edmund Ventura), Timothy Spall (Thomas Tipp), Tilda Swinton (Rebecca Dearborn), Steven Spielberg (guest at David Aames' party) [uncredited].

SLACKERS
Original Film/Destination Films/Alliance Atlantis Communications • 2002

Executive producers: Bradley Jenkel, Mark Morgan, Patrice Theroux; Producers: Erik Feig, Neal H Moritz; Co-producer: Louis G Friedman; Associate producers: Carrie Cook, Dawn Ebert-Byrnes, Shintaro Shimosawa; Director: Dewey Nicks; Screenplay: David H Steinberg; Director of photography: James R Bagdonas; Editing: Tara Timpone; Production design: William Arnold; Original music: Joseph L Altruda, Venus Brown, Justin Stanley.
Cast: Devon Sawa (Dave), Jason Segal (Sam), Laura Prepon (Reanna), Jason Schwartzman (Ethan), Michael C Maronna (Jeff), Cameron Diaz (herself).

THE SWEETEST THING
Columbia TriStar • 2002

Executive producers: Stuart M Besser, Ricky Strauss; Producer: Cathy Konrad; Associate producer: Dixie J Capp; Director: Roger Kumble; Screenplay: Nancy M Pimental; Director of photography: Anthony B Richmond; Editing: David Rennie; Production design: Jon Gary Steele; Music: Ed Shearmur.
Cast: Cameron Diaz (Christina Walters), Christina Applegate (Courtney Rockliffe), Thomas Jane (Peter Donahue), Selma Blair (Jane Burns), Parker Posey (Judy Webb), Jason Bateman (Roger).

GANGS OF NEW YORK

PEA/Miramax • 2002

Executive producers: Maurizio
Grimaldi, Michael Hausman, Harvey
Weinstein; Producers: Alberto
Grimaldi, Martin Scorsese; Co-produc-
er: Joseph P Reidy; Associate producer:
Gerry Robert Byrne; Director: Martin
Scorsese; Screenplay: Jay Cocks,
Kenneth Lonergan, Steven Zaillian
(based on the novel by Herbert
Asbury); Director of photography:
Michael Ballhaus; Editing: Thelma
Schoonmaker; Production design:
Dante Ferretti; Music: Elmer Bernstein.
Cast: Leonardo DiCaprio
(Amsterdam Vallon), Daniel Day-
Lewis (Bill 'The Butcher' Poole),
Cameron Diaz (Jenny), Jim
Broadbent (Tweed), John C Reilly
(Happy Jack), Henry Thomas
(Johnny Sirocco), Liam Neeson
(Priest Vallon).

bibliography

Braun, Liz. 'Something charming about
Diaz'. *Toronto Sun* 28 November 1998.
Christie, Ian (ed). *Gilliam on Gilliam*. Faber
and Faber Limited (London) 1999.
Hobson, Louis B. 'No ordinary life
for Cameron Diaz'. *Calgary Sun* 19
October 1997.
'Everyone's fighting over sultry Cameron
Diaz'. *Calgary Sun* 5 September 1996.
Kirkland, Bruce. 'Something About Dillon
and Diaz'. *Toronto Sun* July 1998.
Morris, Mark. 'Once more with the volume
up'. *The Observer* 20 January 2002.
Pym, John (ed). *Time Out Film Guide,
Ninth Edition*. Penguin (London) 2000.
Slotek, Jim. 'Wedding brings a life less ordi-
nary'. *Toronto Sun* 1 November 1997.
Sterdan, Darryl. 'Good sport'. *Winnipeg Sun*
27 December 1999.
Walker, John. *Halliwell's Film & Video Guide
2001*. HarperCollins (London) 2000.
Wood, Gaby. 'A multitude of Malkovich'.
The Observer 30 September 2001.